UNDERSTANDING
RICHARD POWERS

Understanding Contemporary American Literature
Matthew J. Bruccoli, Series Editor

Volumes on

Edward Albee • Nicholson Baker • John Barth • Donald Barthelme
The Beats • The Black Mountain Poets • Robert Bly
Raymond Carver • Fred Chappell • Chicano Literature
Contemporary American Drama
Contemporary American Horror Fiction
Contemporary American Literary Theory
Contemporary American Science Fiction
Contemporary Chicana Literature
James Dickey • E. L. Doctorow • John Gardner • George Garrett
John Hawkes • Joseph Heller • Lillian Hellman • John Irving
Randall Jarrell • William Kennedy • Jack Kerouac
Ursula K. Le Guin • Denise Levertov • Bernard Malamud
Bobbie Ann Mason • Jill McCorkle • Carson McCullers
W. S. Merwin • Arthur Miller • Toni Morrison's Fiction
Vladimir Nabokov • Gloria Naylor • Joyce Carol Oates
Tim O'Brien • Flannery O'Connor • Cynthia Ozick
Walker Percy • Katherine Anne Porter • Richard Powers
Reynolds Price • Annie Proulx • Thomas Pynchon
Theodore Roethke • Philip Roth • May Sarton
Hubert Selby, Jr. • Mary Lee Settle • Neil Simon
Isaac Bashevis Singer • Jane Smiley • Gary Snyder
William Stafford • Anne Tyler • Kurt Vonnegut
Robert Penn Warren • James Welch
Eudora Welty • Tennessee Williams • August Wilson

UNDERSTANDING
RICHARD POWERS

Joseph Dewey

The University of South Carolina Press

© 2002 University of South Carolina

Cloth edition published by the University of South
Carolina Press, 2002
Paperback edition published in Columbia, South Carolina,
by the University of South Carolina Press, 2008

www.sc.edu/uscpress

Manufactured in the United States of America

17 16 15 14 13 12 11 10 09 08   10 9 8 7 6 5 4 3 2 1

The Library of Congress has cataloged the cloth edition as follows:

Dewey, Joseph, 1957–
   Understanding Richard Powers / Joseph Dewey.
     p. cm. — (Understanding contemporary American literature)
   Includes bibliographical references and index.
   ISBN 1-57003-442-7 (cloth : alk. paper)
   1. Powers, Richard, 1957—Criticism and interpretation.
 I. Title. II. Series.
 PS3566.O92 Z64 2002
 813'.54—dc21   2001007079

Parts of the introduction appeared previously in slightly different form as part of Scribner's American Writers series, edited by Jay Parini. Parts of chapter 4 appeared in slighty different form as part of Dewey, *Novels from Reagan's America: A New Realism* (Gainesville: University Press of Florida, 1999).

CONTENTS

Editor's Preface   vii

Preface   ix

Chapter 1   Understanding Richard Powers   1

Chapter 2   *Three Farmers on Their Way to a Dance*   15

Chapter 3   *Prisoner's Dilemma*   29

Chapter 4   *The Gold Bug Variations*   50

Chapter 5   *Operation Wandering Soul*   70

Chapter 6   *Galatea 2.2*   89

Chapter 7   *Gain*   110

Chapter 8   *Plowing the Dark*   130

Notes   151

Bibliography   163

Index   171

EDITOR'S PREFACE

The volumes of *Understanding Contemporary American Literature* have been planned as guides or companions for students as well as good nonacademic readers. The editor and publisher perceive a need for these volumes because much of the influential contemporary literature makes special demands. Uninitiated readers encounter difficulty in approaching works that depart from the traditional forms and techniques of prose and poetry. Literature relies on conventions, but the conventions keep evolving; new writers form their own conventions—which in time may become familiar. Put simply, *UCAL* provides instruction in how to read certain contemporary writers— identifying and explicating their material, themes, use of language, point of view, structures, symbolism, and responses to experience.

The word *understanding* in the titles was deliberately chosen. Many willing readers lack an adequate understanding of how contemporary literature works; that is, what the author is attempting to express and the means by which it is conveyed. Although the criticism and analysis in the series have been aimed at a level of general accessibility, these introductory volumes are meant to be applied in conjunction with the works they cover. They do not provide a substitute for the works and authors they introduce, but rather prepare the reader for more profitable literary experiences.

M. J. B.

PREFACE

Every professional reader, overtired of shelves of books, reserves the right to recount the story of happening upon a young talent (I emphasize "young" because Powers and I share the same birth year) who is able to revive, once again, the sheer invigorating joy of reading, the intimacy, the wonder that narratives should compel.

Some years ago, my wife was working part-time as a bookkeeper for a small bookstore whose owners needed help painting and varnishing bookshelves. Knocking about the free time that is the special privilege of a teacher's summer, I volunteered—to be paid, I stipulated, by the book of my choice. Browsing through the shelves, I came across a ponderous book that tipped the scales at more than six hundred pages, titled improbably enough *The Gold Bug Variations*. I had never heard of it or its author. Intrigued by the multiple play of puns in the title, I read the first chapter as I stood against the bookshelf I was supposed to be painting. I was hooked in short order and took the book as my payment. I hauled it to the beach that summer to read, then reread, and then relish for one euphoric week during which I was touched personally at a time in my career when, tenured and published, I had all but consigned novels to the arid world of professional activity. Here was a book that stirred deep connections, stunned me with its range of intelligence and wit, yes, but moved me by the sheer power of the stories and the complicated characters it so brilliantly intertwined.

I have since discovered that this is not an unusual reaction to the novels of Richard Powers. Readers feel deeply about his texts, touched by his elegant command of language, his far-ranging erudition, his tremendous feel for the power and pain of the imagination.

PREFACE

As I have come to know his novels—and to a very modest degree the man himself—I have become convinced that here is a genuine talent, all the more tectonic a realization when Powers's age is factored in. This volume is a starting moment, the first large-scale gesture at finding a way through seven of the most innovative, most affective, most daunting novels published in the last fifteen years in American fiction.

I have drawn, of course, from previous work of mine that looked into the work of Powers, and I am grateful for the permission I received to use that work. I am grateful for the kind encouragement of the University of South Carolina Press (specifically Barry Blose, Matthew Bruccoli, and those who so carefully edited the manuscript, Barbara A. Brannon and Jennifer Hynes) and the help of Jay Parini, Irving Malin, and Jim Neilson in getting this volume started. I would also like to thank Rick himself, who is so genuinely accessible and so splendidly personable and who took pains far beyond professional politeness to support this endeavor. And I want to thank my family—my wife, Julie, and my kids, Carolyn and Mark—who justify at every moment Rick's persistent affirmation that it ain't no sin to be glad you're alive.

UNDERSTANDING
RICHARD POWERS

CHAPTER ONE

Understanding Richard Powers

In a literary era that has threatened to make such artifacts quaintly nostalgic, Richard Powers writes big novels of ideas—or more exactly big novels about characters unafraid to tangle with the implications of having ideas and to articulate that remarkable enterprise with wit and erudition.[1] In an era of characters who often struggle to express their sorrows or joys through the limited banality of slang, his characters are remarkably expressive, remarkably thoughtful, their conversation rich with allusions and puns. Yet for all their extraordinary intelligence, they stay remarkably accessible: they bring their intellection to bear as they maneuver—as we all must—through the anxious confusion of relationships and as they deal—as we all ultimately must—with the heavy responsibility of accepting their mortality.

As the signature characters in American literature have always sought, Powers's characters seek to violate the self, to connect. Yet there lurks at the heart of his fiction a haunting loneliness. His characters fall in love—Powers details the difficult dynamic of friendship, courtship, marriage, and family with the humane and generous spirit of the most affective works of contemporary realism—but such affairs of the heart inevitably fall victim to a crushing cycle of expectation and disappointment. Other characters seek to connect to the world through the intellect. Powers has described his characters as "obsessed with the erotics of knowledge."[2] But reprieve from loneliness does not come from cerebral expansion, although Powers confers profound respect on those characters who attempt to command the contemporary world through the exercise of the intelligence. Powers favors professions that wrestle with information: librarians, teachers, scientists, medical students, technical writers, computer wonks, lab technicians, perpetual graduate students. Powers's fictions are often cited (and sometimes criticized) for the dense informational passages on a wide range of highly specialized topics that layer (or clog, depending on the perspective) the unfolding narratives—Powers giving his reader the opportunity to learn about topics that have included game theory, genetic recombination, saponification, corporate economic theory, computer programming, photographic reproduction, polyphonic music, pediatric medicine, tropical botany, and oncology. Yet those characters who attempt to relieve the ache of loneliness through the exercise of the mind are finally limited—they connect, certainly, but to the world, to an "it," and then only through the cold energy of curiosity that leaves them stunned by revelation but nevertheless still stubbornly alone.

Given a world too large to know and too brutish to permit the simple grace of the heart, Powers's defining characters connect most passionately with artifacts of the creative imagination—with odd lines of a poem or an artwork hanging forgotten in a museum, a movement from an esoteric musical work, with a fairy tale heard long ago or some stylish sentimental movie. For Powers, characters moved by the aesthetic connection find in the imagination an expansive and soaring energy all but forgotten in the contemporary era of big-budget Hollywood spectacles, garish audioanimatronic theme parks, the virtual environments of computers, and the tentacled reach of television and video game technologies. Unlike the heart that leaves only the cool sustenance of disappointment, unlike the head that joylessly ties "I" to an "it," the imagination is a potent connecting force that is at once intensely private and splendidly communal as characters

UNDERSTANDING RICHARD POWERS

assume their place within the larger interpretative community of responsive I's (a community that ultimately includes the loneliest figure of all—the reader), working together each and all—and yet staying paradoxically apart.

Such a thematic interest helps position Powers. Given his career-long investigation into the mechanics of the imagination, Powers would seem to fit easily within the postmodern tradition that began at midcentury, works of unnerving lexical daring that investigated with relentless self-awareness the interior worlds fashioned by the unleashed imagination, novels that foregrounded the process of encoding experience into language, often at the expense of developed characters, clear theme, and sustained plot. These daunting texts—performed most notably by Thomas Pynchon, William Gaddis, William Gass, and John Barth—dismissed as irrelevant, even unknowable, the environment outside the imagined as their characters retreated from a world in which the individual had been brutalized into irrelevancy. Thus such texts deliberately, even exuberantly, denied validity to the mimetic premise of the fiction of writers such as John Updike, John O'Hara, William Styron, and John Cheever, realistic fictions that probed the anxieties and benedictions of the ongoing complicated business of living. In his mid-forties Powers is quite aware of his position as a sort of hybrid, a writer whose work consciously attempts to bring together those two schools of fiction. Schooled in the mid-1970s, he clearly respects postmodernism's considerable influence.[3] His novels evidence an audacity in narrative structuring, a fondness for scale, a love of the elaborately terraced sentence, an encyclopedic command of arcane knowledge, a broad use of referents drawn from high and low culture, a fear/fascination with the metaphors of contemporary science, and a keen interest in language and specifically the imperative of tale-telling—each a defining element of much postmodern fiction. Yet few writers in the post-Pynchon era have demonstrated as well a command of the elements of traditional realism: rich storytelling, robust themes, nuanced characters, and an abiding compassion for the dilemmas of such profoundly recognizable characters. Powers sees the two camps as ultimately cooperative: individuals are the stories they tell; like his characters, each individual must narrate his or her world into a shape—language alone creates purpose, direction, dignity. Although not overtly Christian in his writing, Powers is fond of quoting the King James version of Psalm 90: "We spend our years as a tale that is told."

Since 1985 Powers has produced seven novels of unnerving command and grace that have compelled enormous excitement among academics waiting for the first major voice of the post-Pynchon era.[4] Remarkably Powers has no early work that needs to be explained away as an apprentice enterprise. His first novel, *Three Farmers on Their Way to a Dance,* was a National Book Critics Circle Award finalist and won the National Academy and Institution of Arts and Letters Award as well as a special citation from the PEN/Hemingway competition. After his second novel, *Prisoner's Dilemma,* Powers became, at thirty-two, one of the youngest recipients of the MacArthur Foundation "genius" fellowships. His third novel, *The Gold Bug Variations,* also a Circle Award finalist, was tabbed *Time*'s novel of the year. His follow-up work, *Operation Wandering Soul,* was shortlisted for the National Book Award. His next novel, *Gain,* was awarded the 1998 James Fenimore Cooper Prize as the outstanding American work of historical fiction. In that same year Powers was named a fellow of the American Academy of Arts and Sciences for his significant contributions to the exploration of knowledge and culture.

5
UNDERSTANDING RICHARD POWERS

In 1999, just beyond his fortieth birthday, Powers received one of the prestigious Lannan Literary Awards that annually honor "writers of exceptional quality." Powers's novels have already received considerable treatment in academic forums in both the humanities and the sciences and have been translated into a half dozen languages, he has given accomplished and nuanced interviews on the state of contemporary fiction, and his works have generated hot sites on the Internet, not entirely surprising given his background in computer programming and his frequent use of the metaphors of computer science.

Yet, despite his confident deployment of the hip language of computer science, Powers centers his fiction on a theme that has compelled the American imagination since Emerson defiantly declared the self the fittest subject for the literature of the new American enterprise: the irresolvable conflict between the giddy celebration of autonomy and the fearful implication of isolation, the paradox of the imperial, yet terrified self. Well within the mainstream of American literature, from Hester Prynne to Holden Caulfield, from Ishmael to Sethe, from Huck to Harry Angstrom, Powers's characters begin stunned within a vast, emptying loneliness, more particle than part. Their valiant search for connection—so dramatically heightened in a computer age that premises worldwide webbing even as people sit undeniably alone at their terminals—ties Powers specifically to two towering figures whose complementary visions have to a great degree provided structure to American literature: Ralph Waldo Emerson and Emily Dickinson, both of whom Powers regularly glosses. The conflicting visions of Emerson and Dickinson, bold affirmation and the drive to connect on the one hand and anxious questioning and the need to withdraw on the other, very much contest for the heart of Powers's fiction.[5] From one novel to the next, his readers move from affirmation to doubt; the odd-numbered novels celebrate what the even-numbered novels question.

Powers's characters themselves shift between the impulse to connect and its inevitable crash and burn; between the Emersonian urge to embrace the difficult ad-lib of the world and the Dickinsonesque need to recoil from its evident bruising into the supple sanctuary of the aesthetic enterprise, to withdraw into the secured refuge of a novel, a piece of music, a movie house, a museum, even cyberspace. Although long reluctant to encourage the distraction of biography, Powers has lived—like his characters—sustained within a curiously similar geography: never quite at home, never quite comfortable with belonging, shifting between engagement and escape. Powers was born 18 June 1957 in Evanston, Illinois, the fourth of five children, two older sisters and a brother and one younger brother. Early on, in the mid-1960s, his father, a high school principal with a working-class background, moved the family to the north Chicago suburb of Lincolnwood, an older neighborhood, Powers recalls, that was heavily Jewish. "My sisters and brothers and I would be just about the only kids in school for the high holy days." He continues, "I always had a sense that we weren't quite native, a self-image compounded when we moved to Bangkok right before my eleventh birthday." Powers then spent what he has frequently described as five "eye-opening" years in Thailand when his father accepted an appointment with the International School of Bangkok during the height of the American military presence in Southeast Asia. Amid such dramatic relocations, the young Powers discovered the aesthetic sanctuary: he tapped into both a sustaining love of music (an accomplished student of vocal music, he trained in the cello but also plays guitar, clarinet, and saxophone) and a restless curiosity fed by voracious

UNDERSTANDING RICHARD POWERS

reading. He recounts the impact of both the *Iliad* and the *Odyssey* (testimony again to a position between, on the one hand, the realist's impulse to record the world with the historian's eye and, on the other, the poet's privilege to invent with the license of the unleashed imagination). His earliest reading passion, however, was for nonfiction, specifically biographies and science (he has cited particularly the impact of Darwin's *Voyage of the Beagle*—which he read, amazingly enough, in fourth grade). He recalls, in part because of the panicked surge of interest in science following the Sputnik launch, the notion that he was somehow "destined to be a scientist." Thus, as a teenager, he explored careers in paleontology, oceanography, and archaeology before ultimately choosing physics.

In his formal studies, however, Powers would soon find himself pulled between science and the arts. In 1975, he enrolled as a physics major at the University of Illinois. Following a pivotal course, an honors seminar taught by Robert Schneider, a charismatic teacher and an accomplished Freudian critic who Powers recalls convinced him that literature was the "perfect place for someone who wanted the aerial view," he changed to English/rhetoric when he realized, with some frustration, that the sciences demanded, even encouraged, an intolerable specialization.[6] In his literary studies Powers was drawn to the intricate narrative structurings of the first-generation European modernists (particularly the work of Marcel Proust, Thomas Mann, and James Joyce) and to the emotional dramas of Thomas Hardy—again Powers locating himself in between, drawn to both highly experimental modernism with its conception of the novel as a self-justifying architectural form and the compelling tradition of narrative realism that trained the open eye on the world itself. Powers completed his M.A. in late 1979. But the humanities could not provide

Powers a secure space. He elected not to pursue doctoral studies as he feared finding in literary theory and criticism the same limiting need to specialize.

Powers moved to Boston in January 1980 and worked as a computer programmer and freelance data processor, skills he had developed during his off-hours learning the massive computer network systems at Illinois. Computer programmer by day, he continued his eclectic reading program, ingesting volumes of history, sociology, political science, aesthetics, and hard science theory, as well as a wide range of novels and poetry—"random pleasures, all over the map." He lived near the Museum of Fine Arts, where he would spend Saturdays (admission was free before noon), and where, one week, he chanced upon an exhibit that included August Sander's 1914 black-and-white photograph of three Westerwald farmboys heading, according to the title, to a dance. The image haunted Powers. "All of my previous year's random reading just consolidated and converged on this one moment, this image, which seemed to me to [be] the birth photograph of the twentieth century."[7] Within forty-eight hours he quit his job to devote himself to producing his first novel, a project that took more than two years. "I thought: I'm going to put everything that I know in this book, because I'm never going to get another shot at this.... Afterwards, I figured, I'd have to go back and do jobs that people are willing to pay for."[8] That novel, which explores the tectonic impact of artistic images, met with significant critical success, much to Powers's surprise. Encouraged by the realization that he could make a living from writing, Powers moved to southern Holland—in part to withdraw from the distractions of his initial success in the United States but more to immerse himself in that region's fascinating play of multiple languages and dialects and to secure the distance necessary to finish the draft of his second novel, *Prisoner's Dilemma,* an unsettling work that audaciously juxtaposed Disney and the logic of nuclear warfare, a novel that Powers has described as his most American work.

While still in the Netherlands Powers completed his landmark work, *The Gold Bug Variations,* a dense and luminous story of love and death that intricately braids the metaphors of genetics, computer science, and polyphonic music. Two years after *Gold Bug* Powers published the much darker *Operation Wandering Soul,* which chronicled the slow-motion meltdown of a young resident-doctor confronting the harrowing realities of a pediatrics ward in a Los Angeles public hospital. Work on that manuscript was done during a yearlong stay in Cambridge and then completed when Powers returned stateside in 1992 to accept a position as writer-in-residence at the University of Illinois. Powers would use this academic experience to fashion *Galatea 2.2,* an ingenious retelling of the Pygmalion story using a bizarre university computer experiment in which an eccentric neurologist, assisted by a young, successful writer named Richard Powers, attempts to teach a computer network to respond to literature.

This alternating pattern of darkness and affirmation, doubt and celebration—the shifting from Emerson to Dickinson—marks his most recent work as well. In 1998 Powers published *Gain,* a disturbing narrative of an Illinois woman coming to terms at midlife with ovarian cancer most likely caused from the environmental carelessness of a nearby chemical plant, whose two-hundred-year history Powers relates in alternating chapters. But in his follow-up work, the mesmerizing *Plowing the Dark* (2000), Powers chronicles both the grand efforts of a Seattle-based computer research team to produce the first self-contained virtual reality environment and the poignant narrative of an American teacher held hostage for four brutal years by Islamic fundamentalists in Beirut, a prisoner left to the devices of his imagination, the first virtual reality machine.

Named in 1998 to Illinois's endowed Swanlund Chair in English, Powers continues to write, teach, and travel. He is currently completing his eighth novel, a sprawling generational study titled *The Time of Our Singing* (set for 2003), with the properly ambitious themes of racial identity, the iterations of history, and the power of music. The novel will cover more than thirty years of American cultural history during the height of the mid century civil rights movement by centering on the difficult passage to adulthood of the three children of a German Jewish émigré scientist, David Strom, and a black Philadelphia singer, Delia Daley, who marry after a chance meeting during Marian Anderson's epochal 1939 concert on the Washington Mall. At Illinois Powers teaches a graduate seminar in multimedia authoring and an undergraduate course in the mechanics of narrative, and he has undertaken stints at other universities as well. He is far more accessible now than when after his early success his resistance to engaging the public drew comparisons to Pynchon's notorious reclusiveness. After a lifetime of shifting between exotic neighborhoods and diverse cultures, he has found, at midlife, a home at the university—an ivory-tower setting famously existing between engagement and withdrawal, paradoxically a home for the homeless. Despite his evident fondness for Illinois settings, Powers even resists the label of midwestern writer, pointing out that the virtual geography of cyberspace makes such designations strikingly unworkable. "The dream of technology, in large part, is to defeat place, or at least subordinate it to the geography inside us. . . . yet there is nothing, perhaps, more lonely than the consummation of that dream."

UNDERSTANDING RICHARD POWERS

Loneliness, then, haunts Powers's awareness. It is even part of his intricate narrative structures. Powers believes that narrative form is visceral, so that how a story is shaped reveals character and theme. Design always hovers about the reader's awareness. Powers's narratives are each accomplished designs in contrapuntal narration. Two (and sometimes three) narrative braids are offered polyphonically, told side by side, creating a narrative harmony that is as much vertical as it is horizontal (like the staggered lines of "Row, Row, Row Your Boat"). They are narrative lines that do not touch each other, that do not refer to each other, or that are only lightly linked—to the unprepared reader they may initially appear to be entirely incompatible. Yet they come to complement and deepen each other. Narrative structure itself becomes an exercise in his dominant theme: the search for connection among isolates. That search goes further. Each novel defies the terrifying implications of closure by directly inviting the participatory reader to continue the tale, to invent the next episode— writer and reader are joined via the agency of cooperative creation.

Yet such deft structurings are more than gimmicks, more than cool architecture. Powers's passionate vision is keyed to concerns over the individual in the late twentieth century. Although fascinated by the century's boom in science and technology, the humanist Powers raises significant questions concerning the place of the individual amid such dynamic forces. The sheer scale of the techno-world can terrify and compel a withdrawal from its evident brutality and massive facelessness into the clean, simulated spaces of aesthetic refuge, traditionally books and museums but lately movie theaters, computers and other virtual geographies, theme parks, and television. But the reader, responding to the entire reach of Powers's fiction, understands that either impulse—engagement or withdrawal—necessarily draws its urgency from the other; thus each new novel is itself directly linked to questions raised by the previous work, despite not sharing characters or setting or plot, in yet another exercise in connection.

Clearly the odd-numbered books—*Three Farmers, Gold Bug, Galatea 2.2*—are parables of engagement. Vast in intent, they are massively conceived novels, each with a deliberately spacious canvas, narratives of characters rocked, as Emerson so often counseled, by midlife reclamations, characters who come to locate themselves confidently within the broad currents of history, embracing their moment and locating where history has set them down. Each novel is affirmative with the appropriate largeness of Emerson or Whitman. However, the even-numbered books—*Prisoner's Dilemma, Operation Wandering Soul, Gain*—are parables of withdrawal. They are darker novels of characters who stumble about a far more disturbing sense of limitations, often baffled by their history and bruised by experience, novels of wrenching emotional confrontations with the nagging liabilities of our struggle to love and to confront mortality, texts that struggle, as Dickinson did, to adjust to a settling darkness. They are narratives about the terrifying efforts of the self to sustain itself in isolation, about how it creates internal worlds just vast enough for getting lost in. His most recent novel, *Plowing the Dark,* reads like a summary text: it brings together these impulses—Emersonian engagement and Dickinsonesque withdrawal, transcendental connection and anguished loneliness—in a most satisfying contrapuntal fashion.[9]

But even at the narratives' darkest moments, pessimism is never Powers's last word. At the root of his narrative power is the certainty that nothing should create wonder quite so much as articulation itself.

13
UNDERSTANDING RICHARD POWERS

Like the sciences that so fascinated the young Powers, fiction is sufficiently broad to interrogate living itself. Thus, when readers withdraw into one of Powers's novels, they return stunned with new urgency to the deep nuances of living itself. It is a pattern of withdrawal and engagement familiar to any child who has needed the calmative of a bedtime story. Despite Powers's evident intelligence, his fiction has often privileged children's stories as models.[10] Jack and the Beanstalk, Snow White, The Pied Piper, Rapunzel, Sleeping Beauty, Pinocchio, and Maurice Sendak's contemporary classic *Where the Wild Things Are,* as well as lesser-known tales drawn from Far Eastern and Middle Eastern cultures have each centered his novels. Not surprisingly, then, his novels themselves function like children's stories. Reinspired within the space apart that his vast imagination provides, his readers understand like children in the darkling rush of a forbidding evening that with the break of morning they will happily reshoulder the responsibility of living.

Thus what is found in Powers's fiction is a most breathtaking confidence in the self—Powers cannot accept any limiting definition of the individual. The individual cannot be understood—as so much contemporary realistic fiction seeks—solely as a function of domestic relationships or employment or by geography or culture. Rather the individual must be measured by the widest range of contexts—historical, political, technological, aesthetic, sociological, economic, relational, even genetic and molecular. Powers's novels, taken as a whole, work to connect the individual to such a context, to track the lived life using the broadest possible conversation with the widest range of influences. Again and again his novels, flush with the affirmation appropriate to the commencing of a new millennium, reveal how stunning that conversation can prove, how breathtaking connection can be. After a century bent on diminishing the individual amid a colossus of forces whirring about a universe far bigger and emptier than the mind can conceive, Powers cannot accept the endgame of despair nor the logic of cynicism. His is a vision that draws its disarmingly emotional sense of affirmation from the conviction that individuals are bigger than the spare shadow they manage to cast, broader than the love they manage to stir, and deeper than the few lives they manage to touch. His narratives remind readers that they are never as alone, never as apart, as they may feel. Each and all are engaged in the rich ad-lib of the enterprise of living itself, the stunning mystery of animated matter—and that alone justifies affirmation and wonder and demands nothing less than narrative itself to remind people whenever they are most deeply bruised just how fabulous that enterprise is.

CHAPTER TWO
Three Farmers on Their Way to a Dance

Appropriately, Powers's first novel is a gathering of isolates, a bookful of characters who cannot find confidence in the simplest expression of companionship and trust. As if to underscore such loneliness, their three storylines, each intricate and mesmerizing, never touch each other, never refer to each other; chapter to chapter, each tale stays discrete, self-generating, and self-validating. It is only through the agency of the participatory reader that these narrative lines suggest the shared architecture of a plot. The reader notes elements common to each narrative: similar motivations, shared dilemmas, recurring symbols and character types, a steady movement toward similar resolution. Each reader then is assigned a pivotal role in realizing the text. The text thus involves two other unsuspected isolates: Powers, the distant authority deftly weaving these narrative braids; and the reader, compelled to contribute to the narrative's design. In the end all of these isolates in neat, if accidental, conspiracy achieve a cooperative webbing within the aesthetic enterprise itself, each apart yet defiantly a part.

If, as has been suggested earlier, Powers is about the business of connections, he does not tackle here the conventional expression of connection—the anatomy of desire, the anticipations and disappointments of the heart—but rather the dense and complicated obsessions triggered by the imagination, or more specifically by the accidental collision of the active imagination with a suggestive image. In each narrative a character responds deeply and unexpectedly to a black-and-white photograph. In turn Powers depends on a further triggering event—the reader captivated by the narrative itself—to compel a theoretically inexhaustible narrative line. *Three Farmers,* then, opens into a heady Emersonian vastness, a study in the sheer reach of the imagination once it is stunned into deep response.

But it begins with three stories.

The novel privileges with first-person immediacy the story of a nameless drifting, thirtyish stockbroker who in the opening chapter is migrating by train from Illinois to the more promising employment opportunities in Boston. Killing time during a six-hour layover in Detroit (awaiting a *connecting* train), he wanders through the Institute of Arts and happens to see the 1914 August Sander photograph that provides the novel its title. "I knew it at once, though I had never seen it before."[1] Inexplicably dazzled, he finds himself compelled to undertake what becomes a yearlong, self-directed investigation into World War I in an effort to provide some context for his intuitive response to the haunting image of three young men walking through the muddy Prussian countryside on their way to a spring dance shortly before the outbreak of a war that, in its brutality and sheer pointlessness, would mark the birth of the twentieth century.

Eventually despairing over tracking down specific information about the photograph (the museum had misidentified the photographer as an Austrian named "Zander"), he chances to meet during an office Christmas party an elderly cleaning woman, an immigrant named Schreck, who reveals that she knows the photograph. Hazarding the trick of friendship (his initial job review had cited his "standoffishness" [80] as his only shortcoming), he goes to her apartment, scented with rosewater and mothballs, where, amid her "trinkets and

THREE FARMERS ON THEIR WAY TO A DANCE

bangles" (300) from nearly a century of living, she reveals that her dead lover is one of the men in the photo, a framed copy of which she has in her bedroom.

But then she explains. Her lover had died in the war, and she had been left desolate. Before emigrating to America after the war, she had purchased the photo from an "odd German fellow" (305) on a bicycle, most likely Sander himself. To comfort herself for nearly seventy years, she had fashioned out of her need a tie to one of the men who, if she squints and holds the picture closely, resembles her dead lover. Thus the narrator, who begins the novel disdaining the imagination as an "anesthetic, a placebo" (13), is shown a critical insight into its power to console, even connect people amid a century of unprecedented brutalities, heartrending loneliness, and fathomless absurdities. "You've been single your whole life?" the narrator asks. "I wouldn't say that," she replies (304). He thus touches the lure of the empowering imagination, its engine of possibility, its refusal to accept the finality implied by "reality" and its splendid celebration of open-endedness and sheer process. Quite a lesson for a joyless character who admits early on his only vice is "symmetry" (12). He departs her apartment out into the rawness of a January storm suddenly rejuvenated, eager to pore anew over the photograph and to cull from its haunting image his own stories about its characters, most likely the interlacing chapters in this book. As it turns out, then, Powers has been tracking the evolution of a writer.

Against and amid that narrative line runs the romance tale of Peter Mays. He first appears perched precariously on a ledge eight floors over downtown Boston in 1984, watching with casual interest a passing Veterans' Day parade (a holiday, of course, tied to World War I). He chances to glimpse, amid a phalanx of jugglers, vendors, and uniformed soldiers, a stunning redhead toting a clarinet—she is playing Sarah Bernhardt on a float of turn-of-the-century personalities. Like the nameless narrator in that Detroit museum, Peter is "fixed by the temporary and remarkable frame" (35). He is inexplicably driven to track down the mysterious woman who so immediately gives shape and urgency to his otherwise uninspiring career as a technical writer for a computer trade publication. He eventually finds out that the woman is an actress currently staging a one-woman mixed-media show in which she plays a succession of influential women from the last two centuries. Eager to meet her, he arranges to attend a performance. But even as Peter stares at her enormous promotional photos gracing the theater entrance, seeing his mysterious woman posted so publicly deflates his eagerness.

But, during the show, while the actress is rendering Jane Addams, Peter is stunned by a black-and-white photo momentarily projected above the stage of Henry Ford with his arm around a man who looks strikingly like Peter himself. Inexplicably moved by the photo and recalling odd remarks about the inventor made by his mother as he was growing up, Peter returns to his family's Chicago home to search out some explanation. Rummaging through the attic, he uncovers a mysterious envelope that contains a scrap of paper that bears the name "Schreck," a letter signed by Henry Ford, and yet another reproduction of the Sander photo. Ford's letter endows Peter's family with a trust fund tied to the Model T, apparently because one of Peter's relatives, a journalist, impressed the inventor during Ford's ill-conceived 1915 mission to Europe to stop the war. That ancestor, Peter determines, is the middle man in the Sander photograph—Peter Schreck.

THREE FARMERS ON THEIR WAY TO A DANCE

Peter is floored by these revelations. He calculates that the trust fund would now be worth a quarter of a million dollars. Hurrying to Detroit (not coincidentally) to verify his claim, Peter is dismayed to discover that the trust fund is payable only in the counterfeit pennies that Ford had coined bearing his own image, a "fortune" worth exactly two rolls of real pennies. But, along the way, Peter has discovered extraordinary love in the unexpected sincerity and refreshing intelligence of a waitress, Alison Stark, whom he chances to meet during his search for the woman in the parade. Alison's coincidental resemblance to the dead wife of a wealthy eccentric restaurant patron leaves her at novel's end with a tidy inheritance with which the two prepare to begin their own relationship. Denied a counterfeit fortune, he collects presumably authentic riches in Alison Stark.

The third narrative concerns Sander's three farmers themselves, who are named Hubert, Adolphe, and Peter. Powers first re-creates that moment in the Westerwald countryside when the German photographer on a bike stops the three and asks them to pose. Within these chapters, the reader in effect steps into the photograph, into the press and feel, the color and sound, the sheer sensuality of a virtual reality. The three figures, each a different nationality, are networked through an elaborate familial setup of step-relations and cousins. In short, each is given a narrative, an exquisite speculation without foundation within any historic record, the unlicensed exercise of the ignited imagination.

There is the Belgian, Hubert Minuit. He has been sent off to live with relatives in Prussia where, flush with the news of impending war, he abruptly abandons his fourteen-year-old pregnant girlfriend to join his national army in the coming campaign against the Germans.

As he pedals furiously through the open countryside to join the Belgian army, he is shot—ironically, by Belgian engineers demolishing bridges in advance of the Germans. Thus, Hubert becomes the first absurd casualty in what would prove a darkly absurd conflict.

The German, Adolphe, will end up stationed far from the war's hottest action as an officer in charge of managing the occupied Belgian town of Petit Roi. During a routine contraband search, he is drawn by a response to a framed photograph hanging on the wall of a villager's home that depicts a scene from Jack and the Beanstalk (oddly, the cleaning woman has among her knickknacks an antique Jack and the Beanstalk bank). Inexplicably, the image moves him like "slow grace" (142). Despite having the victor's privilege of seizing the photo, Adolphe pays the family for it and keeps it—certain that "the stupid image meant something" (142).

Shortly afterward, following a sniping incident, Adolphe must conduct a harsh town punishment that includes randomly shooting seventy villagers. In short order (in what will become a familiar pattern in Powers's fiction), he short-circuits, leveled by the brutality of the unmediated immediate. He begins to hear what he claims are Russian radio messages via a metal filling in a back molar. When he tries to share this intelligence with his superiors, he is rightly judged delirious. Facing hospitalization, Adolphe flees into the Belgian countryside and is summarily shot through the heart as a deserter. He dies ingloriously, muttering over and over the caption from the photo, "Jack's mother is not pleased with the beans" (228).

The third (the Dutch Peter) survives the war by assuming the identity papers of a Dutch war correspondent who fears being sent to the French front. Peter goes to Paris and, after initially fabricating speculations about the front based on overheard conversations and

THREE FARMERS ON THEIR WAY TO A DANCE

street rumor, comes to take seriously the endeavor to capture "the story of the real war" (271), ultimately venturing to the nearby front and recording with meticulous care the actual words of those soldiers involved in its horror, absurdity, and boredom. Thus another writer evolves. Peter Schreck comes to discover the writer's privileged link to an unnameable but real audience who depend on his eye to record, with disquieting candor, the awkward ad-lib of the unfolding immediate. There is, not surprisingly, little stomach for such realism. The war censors caution Peter that such writing involved the "readers too deeply" (274), a charge that disturbs Peter.

He then turns to the possibilities of the camera as a way to show the human face of the war. He takes a single haunting black-and-white image of a dead soldier abandoned by frazzled medics near a truck carrying the wounded. Not surprising, such immediacy is rejected outright by the censors, who tell him without irony that war photos must not show dead bodies. Undaunted, Peter continues to cover the war (including Henry Ford's Peace Ship enterprise, which apparently validates the photo that will, some seventy years later, compel Peter Mays during his theatre evening and will further link Peter to the narrator's cleaning woman, who claims Peter as a distant cousin). Peter even survives the war—the reader is told that he disappears mysteriously shortly before the outbreak of World War II. His family, hounded by the Nazis, emigrates to America and counts among its descendants Peter Mays.

Importantly, Powers refuses to validate entirely any one story. Chapter to chapter, era to era, no character is entirely secure. There is no irrefutable evidence of which characters are invented and which characters are doing the inventing. Furthermore, the three narratives are each denied conventional closure or any reassuring wrap-up.

UNDERSTANDING RICHARD POWERS

To understand the daring of Powers's narrative, recall that seminal moment in the American literary imagination when Nathaniel Hawthorne's Surveyor, rummaging about the shadowy reaches of the haunted upper room of the Salem Custom-House, finds the rag of scarlet cloth and, holding it up to his bosom, feels the inexplicable warmth of an imagination suddenly surging into expression, suddenly moved to speculate, to violate the sphere of the artifact and to offer a reading of it—and who then boldly invites the reader to do the same. Powers offers both a dense speculation on a photograph and two contrapuntal parables on the power of the imagination to respond intuitively to such a powerful stimulus. He even provides the photo itself on the novel's cover and again on the title page, in effect inviting his readers to weave a tale . . . or two . . . or three. The novel seeks to connect the involved reader with the splendid agitation of response, the bold intrusive activism that has always rested at the mysterious center of the aesthetic exchange. Thus *Three Farmers* braids narratives of characters (including the author and the reader) who each, like Jack with his beans, stumble into unearned wealth and the possibility of magic.

Supremely, then, *Three Farmers* is an Emersonian story of reclamation. When Powers's narrator begins the novel by impulsively deciding to explore Detroit's architectural marvel, the Renaissance Center, he introduces the Emersonian motif of midlife rebirth. For Powers, such resurrection is driven by three energies: the furious kinesis of cerebral expansion; the deep thrust of the needful heart; and ultimately the profound reach of the empowered imagination, both the stunning energy of creativity that bonds passionate artist and participatory audience as well as the measureless ability each person should covet to respond to the artifacts that come to define a culture:

THREE FARMERS ON THEIR WAY TO A DANCE

artwork, music, film, literature. Such response is a breathtaking moment of clarity when, according to the narrator, a "copse of seemingly random trees reveals itself as an orchard" (208). Characters moved by the aesthetic connection find in the imagination a soaring energy that permits a transcendent connection to unnameable others, a place within a larger interpretative community of responsive I's/eyes, working together yet staying stubbornly apart—like the unsettling answer to the traditional child's riddle of St. Ives that figures as the epigraph to the first chapter.

Consider the nameless narrator. The museum epiphany triggers a yearlong voluntary burial within volumes of research material on the generation torched by the Balkan conflict. The narrator is eager to infect his reader with the information bug; thus he includes vivid meditations on the era and its celebrities. Such restless curiosity comes to be the subject of notebooks he keeps, scribbling furiously, as he taps the exhilarating comfort of knowledge, the calming architectural work of propping fact against fact to assemble the edifice of an understandable history, a wonderfully intrusive process renewed, of course, by any individual willing to undertake the demands of learning.

But cerebral expansion, even on the impressive scale mounted by the narrator, is not sufficient. The narrator is frustrated as he comes up against dead ends in his efforts to track down specific information on the haunting photograph. He turns, with considerable hesitation, to others. Socially inept, attending to a job that does not require water-cooler camaraderie or even the occasional interface with clients, subwaying between his office cubicle and his public library carrel, the narrator only grudgingly agrees to attend an office Christmas party. It is not a decision the narrator makes easily—early on he admits that he refuses any job interview that requires sharing personal information. He begins the novel aloof (he turns his office desk so that he faces out the window) and insulated—even from readers. Ironically, given the intimacy of first-person narration, he volunteers little about himself, not even his name (his last name apparently begins with "P"—as a surprise, the cleaning woman fashions that letter on his desk with chocolates). The reader learns only that he has just survived some business failure in Illinois, that his father died too young from cancer, that he disdains automobiles, and that he apparently studied physics. He admits no romantic entanglements or friendships and avoids his nearest neighbors. He shares a sparsely furnished studio apartment only with infesting bugs that, he admits, do not much bother him.

Thus, early in his career, Powers reveals his lack of confidence in the inelegant negotiations between men and women, and thus how lonely his characters are. The heart too often misleads—consider the crude sexual misadventures of the three farmers themselves. Such distrust of the heart renders problematic whatever faith the reader may want to place in the deliberately improbable romance that develops between Peter Mays and Alison Stark. But Powers does not abandon the considerable pull of others. Over and over, benevolent strangers intrude and, by extension, forge an Emersonian network of ties, the dimensions of which the characters themselves only begin to suspect. At critical moments Peter Schreck, Peter Mays, and the nameless narrator are each dramatically helped by total strangers, recalling Ford's motto, inscribed on his pennies: "Help the Other Fellow." To suggest this elastic webbing, Powers deploys suggestive metaphors for connections that bind strangers: the stock market; newspapers and magazines; theatre and film productions; art museums; complicated

THREE FARMERS ON THEIR WAY TO A DANCE

extended families; bus and subway systems; computer networks; even World War I itself, both in the grim inclusivity of a civilian war and in the ghastly exercise in interdependence taught by Adolphe's occupational force in Petit Roi when it punishes the entire community for the actions of a splinter resistance faction. In a century in which the individual has been reduced to irrelevance (during his Detroit layover the narrator studies a fearful Diego Rivera mural in which workers are eerily dehumanized), Powers rejects such diminishment. Everything—every event, every person—is tied in unintentional, undirected, unsuspected choreography, like the tumbling of colored rocks recovering design within a kaleidoscope tube. Like the simple beans that even Jack at first disparages, the individual is consequential in ways he or she does not begin to suspect.[2]

Thus, within the formidable magic of the Christmas season, the narrator introduces himself to the immigrant office cleaning woman, a stranger, who alone will complete the search that has given his narrowed life sudden depth and clarity. It is a linkage the narrator initially resists. After the Christmas party, fearing the terrible vulnerability of accepting the intrusive presence of another, the narrator awkwardly avoids the cleaning woman. Almost reluctantly, while out walking in a gathering mid-January storm, he finds himself heading to the old woman's apartment. In that slender gesture he will find the luminous comfort of confluence as the woman shares with him the heavy sorrow of her bruised heart and her own complicated connection to the haunting Sander photograph. They end the afternoon joyously improvising harmonies to the tinkling of her broken-down player piano, a fitting tableau of connections: his voice and hers as well as the effortless cooperation of full-throated humanity with mechanical technology.

It is that moment of reclamation and connection that opens for the narrator the fullest interior energy—his own imagination—and frees him from his ruthlessly one-dimensional search for information about the photo. As he departs, he realizes in a liberating jolt that the imagination empowers him to create a reading of the photo ("the form that delights the eye prescribes action" [336]), a reading that will in turn join him to countless others who have found themselves similarly mesmerized, each taking from the original but nevertheless enlarging it. With Emersonian resonance, the narrator, who begins the book plagued by motion sickness, closes celebrating the vibrant flux of a wild horizon opened by the imagination. The novel itself will end with one of Peter Mays's colleagues, a man particularly dull-eyed and suspicious of depth, suddenly crashing through the barricade of potted plants around his desk because he is inexplicably drawn to examine the print of the Sander photograph that Peter has left on his desk.

But Powers saves the deepest invitation for the reader. With the audacity of a first-time novelist, Powers leaves open each of the narrative lines, thus sharing with his reader the usually closed-off sphere of a novel's creative center. That reader must collaborate in the novel's fullest creation. Powers offers an appealing metaphor for this cooperation. Rummaging about his attic, Peter Mays comes across an old stereoscope and a box of stereoscopic photographs, which enjoyed a faddish rage in the early days of photography. With the handheld viewer, a forerunner of the modern ViewMaster, two-dimensional photos, placed side by side, are suddenly coaxed into the living magic of a third dimension, suggesting the cooperative enterprise of the artist and audience coaxing to its fullest life the otherwise lifeless artifact, whether paint on canvas, images in a photograph,

THREE FARMERS ON THEIR WAY TO A DANCE

notes on a sheet of music, words pronounced in a theatre, or ink lines pressed onto paper.[3]

Thus Powers (or perhaps the narrator) offers multiple endings for Peter Schreck's family and its emigration route to America even as the reader is cautioned against accepting any as final. The reader is further asked to build on the tantalizing possibility of a happy ending tendered to Peter Mays and Alison Stark, despite their being virtual strangers and bound only by the Preston Sturges–styled wacky escapade of an improbable bogus inheritance.[4] The narrator himself prepares to cast free of his anchorage in the second-floor history section in the neighborhood library for the deeper reward of spinning his own tales, like Hawthorne's Surveyor who himself celebrates his own dismissal from a narrow ledger occupation in the Custom-House to recline at fireside and to allow his fancy at last its flight.

In this freshman outing Powers freely abdicates his privilege of authority. Wide-eyed and flushed with sudden empowerment, the reader must continue the fluid narrative. The great benefit of the machine age, Powers's narrator argues in an arresting set piece on photography, is the ready availability of art, the ease with which reproduction technologies have made artifacts—from music to film to art prints to books—available to an ever-expanding community.[5] The aesthetic response is no longer the sole privilege of the affluent. Everyone can all join the round. To participate in any artifact is to change it, renew it, and keep it—and the participant—viable. Powers depends on a participatory reader to depart *Three Farmers* inspired by the same intoxicating possibility that stuns each of his characters. To live unaware of the tectonic force of the imagination is untenable— the photo that so moves Adolphe shows Jack and his mother melodramatically despairing over the beans. Interestingly, the theatre Peter Mays attends is Your Move Theatre.

But Powers understands that such cooperation is unsettlingly fragile, uneasily virtual—artist and audience never realize any actual confluence. Furthermore, by placing so much narrative emphasis on a particularly bloody and pointless war, Powers shows that the aesthetic enterprise can easily be dismissed as precious, artists busily shaping design, line, and color amid a most gruesome twentieth century, every artist like August Sander busily carting his cumbersome camera about a European countryside that is about to ignite.

But here, giddy as perhaps only a first-time novelist can be,[6] Powers reminds readers of the inexplicable binding of artist and audience and encourages them ultimately to test their own aesthetic impulse, to respond, for instance, to the shadows, colors, and lines of a work of art or to listen to the intricate movement of a musical piece or to find themselves engaged by made-up characters doing made-up things—to touch what Powers's narrator terms the "instant of aha" (208). To borrow from the Emily Dickinson couplet, itself uncharacteristically Emersonian in its bravura, quoted during the theatre performance Peter Mays attends, "I dwell in possibility/A fairer house than prose" (195). Imagination connects—character to character, author to characters, reader to characters, reader to author, and ultimately readers to readers—by endowing with authenticity the rich fabulation of inexhaustible creativity. Yet even as the reader closes the novel, entirely taken by the spectacle of the reaching imagination, there lingers uncertainty over the implications of such wholesale retreat. Not surprisingly, in his follow-up work, Powers will turn back to the bruising real world to scour its anxious terrain to justify some similar sense of affirmation.

CHAPTER THREE
Prisoner's Dilemma

The reader first meets Eddie Hobson stretched out with his four grown children on the hard ground on a harsh November night. Together, they canvass the night sky, and, with the help of Eddie's feeble flashlight, they carefully trace familiar constellations. It is a telling moment—the forbidding vastness of the universe (as defined by the sciences of the last century with its terrifying implication of humanity's puniness) triggers the need to indulge the pleasant nostalgia of pretty pictures amid light-years of chilly emptiness. Such fragile configurations, of course, are fictions, bravura acts of the imagination in anxious retreat from the disturbing implications of the immediate. Like Powers's first novel, his second, the startlingly dense *Prisoner's Dilemma* (1988), foregrounds the engine of the imagination. Yet it provides a necessary counterargument to the refulgent vision of *Three Farmers*. This sophomore work cautions that the imagination, for all its energy, can isolate individuals from a reality that they too easily abandon, forgetting how deeply the world justifies wonder.

Like Powers's first work, *Prisoner's Dilemma* is an architectural complex of three loosely related narrative lines. The most accessible story, told in twenty-one numbered chapters, centers on the Hobson family of De Kalb, Illinois. Each chapter is controlled by the perceptions of one family member. Only the father, despite being the emotional center of the family, is denied such access. Eddie Hobson, a high school history teacher, is a charismatic paterfamilias, a compendium of factoids who with a perpetual "smart-ass grin"[1] challenges his kids at the dinner table with logic problems and whose most trivial conversation sparkles with puns, aphorisms, and allusions. Eddie believes in the sheer muscle of intellection and counsels his kids that the "only hope of salvation lay in finding out where history dropped you down" (50). The more people know, he assures them, the less they can be hurt.

Brave talk, it turns out, from one leveled by his own brief brush with history.[2] Eddie has suffered for some thirty years from radiation poisoning triggered, Powers reveals late in the novel, while he is on assignment at an obscure Air Force outpost near Alamogordo, New Mexico. After excusing himself for a smoke after an all-night card game, he witnessed, unprotected, that first blast of the atomic age. Like Eddie, the family has long resisted confronting the obvious symptoms—fainting spells, hair loss, vomiting, lumps and lesions in Eddie's armpits, bleeding gums, constant fatigue, severe weight loss. But as the novel opens and the family gathers shortly before Thanksgiving to celebrate the youngest son's eighteenth birthday, they can no longer ignore how sick the father is.

Agreeing to check himself into a Chicago veterans' hospital just before Christmas, Eddie is no sooner admitted to face a battery of exploratory tests than he checks himself out and, via cryptic phone calls to his worried family, reveals that he is returning to the New Mexico site where history so brutalized him. The youngest son, Eddie Jr., impulsively rents a car to pursue the father. Although he finds evidence at Los Alamos that his father had been there, the son finds no trace of the father. He assumes (as the reader does) that his father is gone, dead at fifty-two—perhaps a suicide, perhaps a natural death. No body is ever recovered.

PRISONER'S DILEMMA

Interspersed among the chapters chronicling Eddie's slow-motion dying are italicized sections that provide the other two narrative threads. One set, each chapter headed by a year, is a fantastic mock-historic narrative in which Walt Disney, eager to help in the propaganda effort during World War II, conceives of an experimental cinematic project designed to inspire heroic optimism in the home front. This project, which evolves into a populist epic that would be a cross between Frank Capra's *It's a Wonderful Life* and Disney's own *Fantasia,* would involve a revolutionary splicing of animation and live action. A young boy would find himself ably guided by Mickey Mouse, a mentoring spirit who would reassure the boy as he grows up that his life—and by extension the reader's—mattered despite personal setbacks and despite the enveloping darkness of this horrific century with its absurd escalation toward self-extermination. But such unearned optimism troubles the reader. During the film's projected closing reel, after witnessing a disturbing wasteland spectacle of legions surrendered to alienation, bunkered within locked homes, and willingly abdicating the "common project of being alive" (310), Eddie simply whispers, "*Fairy Dust. . . . Only believe*" (312).

The project nevertheless acquires substantial government funding, with which Disney constructs a massive soundstage amid the rural emptiness of Illinois (coincidentally near De Kalb). He then mans it with ten thousand film technicians he liberates from among the more than one hundred thousand Japanese Americans interred in government camps hastily constructed along the Pacific coast after Pearl Harbor. Disney eventually casts a young Eddie Hobson to play the starry-eyed central figure; several of the film's early scenes are drawn from Eddie's New Jersey childhood. But the film is never completed. At war's end Disney abandons the project to head to California to build a vast theme park, a culture's playscape safe from the implications of a world moving apparently inexplicably toward elective holocaust. Disney is last seen quoting into his ever-present dictaphone from Boccaccio's *Decameron*—a disturbing passage that sanctions escape from a threatening and threatened environment.

The other italicized chapters, each headed by a phrase, are more problematic. Presumably, these chapters track the Hobsons' oldest son, Artie, a twenty-five-year-old law student, as he sorts through his father's effects after the flight to New Mexico. The troubled manchild struggles to piece together some sense of a father who, despite evident love for his kids, never quite managed the trick of closeness or the warmth of intimacy. Artie provides critical background to Eddie, creatively ruminating about the enigmatic father, an exercise in imaginative speculation, both intrusive and empowering, that recalls similar efforts by the nameless narrator and the elderly cleaning woman of *Three Farmers*. Artie reconstructs the young Eddie's epiphanic visit at age thirteen to the spectacular pavilions of the 1939 New York World's Fair; the devastating impact of his older brother's wartime death in a fluke training accident while in the Army Air Corps; the comically eccentric courtship of Artie's mother; the brutal collision with history at Trinity. Most important, the reader finds out about the father's eccentric thirty-year project—happily dictating into an ancient tape recorder, behind locked doors and under a photo of a brooding Disney, the particulars of a fantastic private world he calls Hobstown, based on the hugely popular General Electric Futurama exhibit at the World's Fair, an impressive series of intricate scale-model landscapes meant to suggest the future growth of cities.

PRISONER'S DILEMMA

After Eddie's death, however, Artie finds that his father's neatly labeled reel-to-reel tapes have been erased, save one. The reader surmises that the interspersed Disney chapters have been the transcript of Eddie's sole surviving tape, which, apparently, the kids have been listening to. Each family member then steps to the microphone to offer a take on the father's last weeks, dictations that the reader most likely has been reading in the nonitalicized chapters. Collectively the family struggles to create a presence from a disturbing absence, working to assemble some cohesive picture of this distant father who himself struggled against the darkest implications of post-Hiroshima America.

As in *Three Farmers* narrative authority is never entirely confirmed. We never know who is telling which story, which story (if any) participates in what we might term narrative reality, or which story is being generated by which character. Tale-telling is both foregrounded and undercut. The narrative construction here is further complicated (and undercut) by a cameo appearance at novel's end by Richard Powers himself, a teenager reeling from the too-early death of his father from cancer (the faded photo on the dust jacket of the hardcover edition is the Powers family). In a bold stroke of imaginative restoration, Eddie Hobson himself returns as an apparition who nonchalantly rejoins the family dinner table to deal a game of cards. Is *Prisoner's Dilemma* then a painful realistic memoir of a troubled son and a haunted family struggling to understand the distances that remain between themselves and an eccentric father, a man victimized by the tectonic blow of history? Or is this a rollicking, decidedly postmodern de/reconstruction of the seductive (melo)dramatic theater of hot and cold war that uses—and parodies—both that generation's sitcom expectations of the suburban family and its embrace of escapist entertainment, suggested by Disney's midcentury move to the cultural center of American life?

Not surprisingly, it is something in between. *Prisoner's Dilemma* provides a sobering counterbalance to the giddy exuberance of *Three Farmers*. Powers's second novel cautions that, despite the persuasive possibilities of the imagination suggested by Powers's first novel-qua-fairy tale, if the imagination empowers it imprisons as well. *Prisoner's Dilemma* plays on the tension between captivity and freedom; a recurring line within the narrative asks, "How free are we?" Here Powers's focal character is not the ever-retreating figure of the poisoned father (he remains as inaccessible to the reader as he is to his family). Rather, Powers positions at the narrative's redemptive center the youngest son, who comes finally—in a defiant gesture decidedly lacking in the first novel and among the other Hobsons—to affirm the terrible beauty of the unscripted real world. This work suggests that Powers himself is not entirely content with the bold resolution of *Three Farmers*. To borrow from the Dickinson poem that shapes the argument of that first work, here the reader discovers that, dwelling in possibility notwithstanding, prose is a pretty fair house as well.

Unlike the nameless narrator who finds himself ultimately enclosed within a luminous webbing of unexpected connections, Eddie Hobson offers a counterfable of disconnection. Much as Jack and the Beanstalk thematically centers *Three Farmers,* Snow White, a far darker tale that figures in a number of scenes in *Prisoner's Dilemma,* serves as the suggestive center of this work. In that tale a distressed character on the run is victimized by the inexplicable animosity of a life-threatening figure-force, is poisoned after the sole encounter with that malevolent force, and then is chilled into protective hibernation

PRISONER'S DILEMMA

(suggested in the Disney animated classic by the glass casket fashioned by the dwarfs), a public entombment that ends only with the daring intervention of a significant other. Clearly Eddie is the Snow White figure who never quite finds the way to connection, much less revival. Thus he comes to the reader casketed, so near yet so distant, so apparently lifelike yet suspended in a haunted anti-life. Despite glibly mouthing Emerson's rhetoric of self-empowerment, Eddie with his fearful heart is as anxious as Dickinson within her sanctuarial bedroom. Like Dickinson, indeed like all artists (including the narrator of *Three Farmers*), Eddie is a frustrated control freak (while on vacation, he scavenges the beach for driftwood with such doggedness that his son compares him to Melville's relentless Ahab), within a century that has spun wildly free of such logic.

Powers uses Eddie's troubled life to expose the infinite strategies twentieth-century humanity has come to adopt to avoid engaging a century that has, in its evident barbarity, justified retreat. Thus for all his attractive intelligence and brash bravura, Eddie Hobson is a monitory character. Readers cannot afford—nor does Powers endorse—his solution of withdrawal. Eddie has too easily surrendered—as his hunched back and his fondness for alcohol suggest. Two events—his brother's accidental death and the noiseless flash at Trinity Test Site—have only taught Eddie the inconsequentiality of the vulnerable individual. When Artie considers the magnificent premise of the so-called Butterfly Effect, the foundational assumption of chaos theory that argues that given significant investigation the smallest event leads to unsuspected grand-scale consequences, he introduces a compelling Emersonian argument that the father has abandoned. And, like Eddie, struggling against the evidence of the atrocities so casually conducted during World War II and the eerie wonderland logic of Mutual Assured Destruction, in which a generation of defense strategists artfully argued that nuclear weapons had redefined war as species suicide even as they drew up plans for just such a war, twentieth-century humanity has too easily indulged pleasure prisons that offer what such strategic withdrawals have offered since Boccaccio: protective isolation at a civilization's crisis moment.[3]

Theme parks and movie theaters, game boards and department stores, televisions and libraries, classrooms and locked homes—Powers introduces each as a tidy strategy of interment, each an enclosed carnival playscape. Powers argues that virtually any text produced by the post-Hiroshima imagination is essentially a captivity narrative, that the sheer reach of nuclear weaponry has in effect imprisoned humanity itself within the alogic of a species that has plotted to survive only by exterminating itself. Tora, Powers argues, has compelled Tara. And, as with the Stockholm Syndrome (to which Powers refers), humanity has come to love what imprisons it: twentieth-century culture has come to relish the privileged management, the graceful logic and clean efficiency of such playscapes. The participatory reader, a prisoner of the same dilemma, must come to realize that such retreat is an unbecoming posture—recall the adult daughter Lily crouching in strained discomfort in a bigger-than-life backyard dollhouse.

Thus, within this narrative, Powers moves from prison to prison, from one enclosure to another: the Japanese American relocation camps along the Pacific coast, the colossal soundstage that Disney calls into being amid the Illinois wastes, the spectacular General Electric pavilion at the World's Fair. The reader eavesdrops on Disney's resolve to create an unprecedented entertainment complex outside Anaheim and hears about (although, of course, never visits) Eddie's lexical playscape, the virtual reality site he dubs Hobstown.

37
PRISONER'S DILEMMA

In addition, the reader is shuffled in and out of the pleasure dome of the darkened movie theater, watching escapist fare such as *The Wizard of Oz, It's a Wonderful Life, Orchestra Wives, Gone with the Wind, A Christmas Carol, Fantasia,* Busby Berkeley's frothy musicals, and, of course, Disney's *Snow White*.

There are other, less obvious prisons in that humanity has gratefully indulged. In downtown Chicago the Hobsons thrill to the department-store windows of Marshall Field's, each one a crafted life-sized diorama of a Christmas from the past. At the veterans' hospital, with dying patients strapped to cables and tubes, the untidy terror of mortality is antiseptically refashioned into the presentable—as Artie observes, "Death used to be a horrible, demanding, agonizing, nauseating ordeal. . . . But his [father's] era had at last taken care of it, turned it into a level spot on a graph, a rounded decimal" (254). In his history classroom Eddie Hobson has spent a career deftly packaging the chaos of events into tidy accessible eras. At home he teases his grown children with riddles—each a cozy Q-and-A game structure that rewards the exercise of the mind with the benediction of solution. The Hobsons themselves play elaborate board games, hold endless rounds of card games, and even invent dinner table games. The sons toss a football in tight, precise patterns. The sisters dabble with a Ouija board. They are all voracious readers. The father encourages the children to learn, believing that, within encyclopedias, the individual rests invulnerable.

This strategy of willed disconnection makes for a forbidding narrative. Unlike Powers's first narrative, which expands with every breathtaking chapter, here the narrative is claustrophobic and airless. Interred within so many attractive prisons, readers may not realize how elaborate, how strangling are such edifices, nor how desperate is our dilemma as an imprisoned reader. Powers strings the narrative with barbed wire (including a visit to the De Kalb restored historic homestead where its inventor lived). He isolates his characters—although the family Hobson is a loving unit (they are given to impromptu sing-alongs and rib each other with enviable gentleness), their love is necessarily exclusionary. They have lived a harsh gypsy life (Eddie's fainting spells and unconventional teaching style made him a problematic hire, and the family has relocated four times). In De Kalb they have acquired no friends—Eddie is currently feuding with his neighbors because he refuses to rake his wide lawn. But more disturbing, they are even uneasy with each other. They find difficult the simplest gesture of honest talk—their conversations are snappy, pun-riddled, and erudite but often maddeningly artificial. Even their chapters read as discrete narratives, each member neatly sectioned off from the others. The family's most pressing issue—the father's health—is seldom addressed directly: "no one ever spoke a word of what was going on out loud" (30). The daughters, for instance, consult a Ouija board at one point and at another conduct a circuitous conversation about what to do about Eddie by typing alternating lines on an ancient Olympia typewriter. Thus, if the family maintains an enviable harmony, it is constructed on the seductive logic of disconnection that Powers cannot finally endorse.

To reveal the damage such disconnection inflicts, Powers uses the father, or rather the Eddie as reconstructed by his son. Insight has clearly not led to clear sight. The flash at Alamogordo has blinded Eddie. His brave strategy of containing life through the intellect, a strategy as old as Newton but made dangerously nostalgic in the twentieth century, masks his anxieties and only makes glamorous his helplessness. He is distanced from his family, inaccessible to the simplest chitchat. Entombed in his back room fashioning his ghost town, the Great Dictator, as he is called by his son, has learned only to justify

PRISONER'S DILEMMA

disconnection. Eddie distances himself from the two experiences that alone make people fully human: the gentle terrorism of love and the sweet fascism of death. When Eddie decides as a teenager that it is time to marry, he refuses to date—a process he sees as too vulnerable to chance—and rather calculates his needs and then goes shopping for the right woman as if he is picking out an appliance. And, despite being exposed to radiation in 1945, Eddie denies his illness until just days before his death in 1978. Stunned by the fluke death of his brother, by the clumsy intrusion of chance, terrorized by the implications of his own uneasy era, shaken by the depth of death in his sorry century, poisoned like Snow White, Eddie retreats into the false invulnerability of isolation for more than thirty years.

Not surprisingly, the family members, so imprisoned by his personality, are each Snow Whites as well. At twenty-five, Artie is entowered within the protective confines of law school. His prolonged tenure as a professional student is uncomplicated by friends or by romantic entanglements. He acknowledges the uneasy relief he feels when infrequent weekend trips home are over and he can leave behind the troubling complications of his dying father and return to the sanctuary of law school. As a lawyer he will neatly (and entirely arbitrarily) domesticate the mess of his clients' emotional interactions into the attractive neatness and the wholly artificial plot of sworn affidavits. In the closing chapter Artie erases his father's only Hobstown tape to begin his own virtual reality, constituting a brand new lexical playscape, this one about a model family in a model home, an exercise that indicates his father's fondness for withdrawal has indeed passed to his eldest son.

Eddie's daughters have pursued similar retreats. Forsaking college, Rachel has found her own tender magic kingdom as a CPA coolly working out actuarial tables—artfully packaging the messy data of the patternless stroke of mortality into the mock-precision of attractive tables. Early on Lily, the older sister, appears to promise engagement. She earns a degree in special education, a career that would demand generous involvement in often heartbreaking experiences amid genetic mishaps. In her university days she undertakes modest protests late in the Vietnam era. But she never completes her degree, and the passion for activism falls of its own uselessness. She marries, she says, because she is pleased by the alliteration of her married name (Lily Leeds), the earnest work of love reduced to an Eddie-esque word game. The marriage proves a disaster. When the husband's physical abuse compels her within a year to retreat to the safe refuge of home, careerless, she maintains a curious epistolary non-relationship with a neighbor, an elderly woman who lives alone and whose daily routine Lily watches with peculiar fascination. The letters ("unpostable" [207]) are rich speculations about the woman spun only within the cool intimacy of Lily's imagination. She never offers the woman even the simplest greeting.

Ailene, the mother, has sacrificed any concern for herself amid years of tending to the eccentricities of her damaged husband and keeping together a family during their "descent into gypsyhood" (122). She distrusts complexities—she never went to college; she embraces the simple logic of the Golden Rule; she disdains her husband's "noxious, logical knots" (117). Alone at the kitchen table, as she prepares yet another shopping list, she begins absently to scribble bits of her own life story. Such tentative explorations, however, quickly shut down—she quietly erases even these fragments. Thus the reader learns next to nothing about this woman as she tends to her domestic routines within a "paper-towel prison" (117) among spotless counters and gurgling coffeepots, her own controlled space, her own magic kingdom.

41
PRISONER'S DILEMMA

This, then, is the Hobson clan—each casketed like Snow White, each self-imprisoned, each a solo nation. Eddie is fond of a classic one-liner: "All Indians walk in single file. At least the one I saw did." Each Hobson is seduced by the suasion of magic-kingdom logic, overwhelmed by the evident agonies of circumstances and willingly accepting a lifestyle that sanctions withdrawal into private worlds, or wholesale retreat and simple disengagement, and/or the creative use of the imagination to make comfortable that apart-ness. Isolated within their loving family sanctuary, the Hobsons never trouble the implications of this wholesale retreat, the depth of their shared dilemma.

Yet if Powers inters, he also frees. With Emersonian largeness he offers the exception of the youngest Hobson, Eddie Jr. His example recalls the two forebears who provide such powerful glosses within *Prisoner's Dilemma:* Capra's George Bailey and Dickens's Ebenezer Scrooge. The narrative works to free the youngest Hobson by allowing him to reclaim, like those two characters, what his family has so willfully rejected: the dignity of an individual worth celebrating and our necessary place among others. But, unlike Capra and Dickens, Powers is no sentimentalist. The young son must journey to ground zero of the twentieth century, to the Trinity Test Site. There he hears a tape his father leaves behind of his singing a rendition of Vernon Dalhart's forlorn 1920s hillbilly folk ballad, "The Prisoner's Song," about a poor man separated from his love and serving time for vagrancy, which includes a terrifying line that summarizes for the son the deep sorrow of the father—and by extension of this century: "*I wish I had someone to trust in / For I'm tired of living alone*" (340).

In an epiphanic flash akin to his father's revelation years earlier at the same site, Eddie Jr. grasps his father in a way the other Hobsons do not. He understands the man's vast loneliness, his terror over his inability to trust love, his cynical retreat into an inviolable sanctuary. He also understands that his father must serve as a caution. The son picks up a handful of the hot white sand—into which the father has so inelegantly disappeared—and tosses the "unworldly crystals" (341) high into the air and imagines they circulate the globe and sting awake sleepers' eyes, a gesture that recalls the revival strategies of both Emerson's and Whitman's more exuberant writings. Earlier, when Eddie Jr. decides (not surprisingly against the counsel of the family) to follow the runaway father, to depart their sanctuarial home and step out into a howling winter storm in a gesture of impulsive engagement, Eddie flashes to his brother a brave "transcendental grin" (305).

This Eddie assures the reader that his father has been victimized by a faulty dilemma, the too-easy notion that humanity has only two choices: to engage the world and discover the horrors of its unfolding chaos or to escape its pressure by indulging pixie-dusted magic kingdoms and there sustain a bogus hope that feeds on our anxieties. It is the son who suggests, quite radically, that engagement can lead to wonder and that hope need not be saccharine impossibilities. As Disney ironically speculates in the midst of World War II, "*The side that comes through this final fight still loving the exhausted, ruined world, the side with more delight, will be the winning side*" (102–3).

Eddie alone touches such delight. He is clearly not like the other Hobsons. At eighteen, he is the last born and is much younger. His brother describes him as "genuinely happy, gripeless" (170). A teenager surrounded by adults, he presumes the privilege of maturation and the expectation of evolution denied his older siblings, who have established identities and clear futures. Importantly, he is not their intellectual equal—he cannot compete in their marathon trivial pursuits and maintains a modest academic standing in high school (when his girlfriend, who is much smarter, quotes Rabelais, he assumes it is an old boyfriend). He is uncertain with words, the very medium his father so deftly manipulates. He pronounces "epitome" as it is spelled, admits to not knowing words his girlfriend uses in conversation, and suggests that big words are primarily useful for the SAT.

But Eddie Jr. evidences—for the first time in Powers's fiction—a capacity for sympathy, what his older brother, himself something of a misanthrope, terms an "alarming propensity for making friends" (90). Amid his family's elaborate dodge of ignoring the father's illness, Eddie asks why the family does not simply take the man to a doctor. Not surprisingly, it is Eddie who impulsively rents a car to pursue, without much hope of success, a father who wants only to get lost. Amid a family of self-interred eccentrics Eddie maintains a healthy social life. He is a joiner, a social animal. He is the family's only jock, by definition a team player. He is the kind of guy who would sooner swallow phlegm than "offend anyone by spitting" (89). He has a girlfriend (whose supple waist floods him with delectation) and a coterie of buddies (at novel's end Eddie is bound for a notorious party college downstate). Eddie Jr. then both is/is not a Hobson (after all, he does not know the meaning of either "curmudgeon" or "sequestered," both words critical to a Hobson)—and that allows him the opportunity to break the seductive matrix of the family and thus to command (despite his slender presence amid the far flashier Hobsons) the redemptive center of the novel.

What lessons does Eddie Jr. offer? They are significant not only because they balance the Hobsons' strategies of interment but also because they act as correctives to the similar resolution suggested by the nameless narrator in *Three Farmers*. Eddie reminds the reader of what gives worth to the world that so terrorizes the father (and that never quite sparkles for the nameless narrator): the irrational risk of love, the reassuring animation of the organic earth, and the selfless gesture of caring.

Eddie Jr. is given only one chapter,[4] which follows his first date with a pretty junior named Sarah, a night in which he touches with unexpected certainty the unrehearsed immediacy of potent attraction, the electric thrill of sensuality, and the sacramental simplicity of the heart. The two laugh, kiss, hold hands, tease, talk, confide in each other. It is the (extra)ordinary experience of (un)common love. The date follows like some corny old movie. Importantly, however, unlike his father's tightly scripted courtship, this is unmediated experience. Eddie and Sarah begin their chapter by leaving a movie theater, stepping away from a magic kingdom (they have watched *Fantasia*) and into the sweet tumble of the expressed heart. When Eddie alludes to *It's a Wonderful Life,* Sarah (refreshingly) does not even know the film, and Eddie admits that he has not actually seen all the movies he knows about.

But Eddie does not only celebrate the rich pull of love. During the date, he speaks with infectious enthusiasm about the tonic effect of nature. Eddie makes a fuss over a simple mushroom (in striking contrast to his father's encounter with a mushroom of a far different sort) and how in the coming spring rain will trickle down the slender trees and pool on the cool ground thus making possible the tidy miracle of fungi. It is a glowing Emersonian appreciation of the great cycles of biological life that wheel so furiously—and unacknowledged— all about and that defy with splendid resiliency the iron inevitability of nuclear apocalypse.[5] He admits to turning over rocks and eagerly watching the fury of insect life. He admits that had he the grades he

PRISONER'S DILEMMA

would be an entomologist, that he would study life "for hours without blinking" (197). But if he has not the brains of a scientist (which, given the evidence of his family, may actually be fortunate), he clearly has the generous open eye of one. His appreciation for the sheer scale of living, its relentless argument of inexhaustibility, and its shatteringly precise design—all of it fashioned by the blind work of chance and all subject to the inevitable stroke of death—puts him at radical distance from the other, entombed Hobsons. Think of it, he says, "all these combinations, under our feet. The size of it. The possibilities" (197).

In confiding to Sarah about his ailing father (a gesture of confidentiality that signals the depth of his need for others), Eddie points out insightfully that his father is a sentimentalist trapped by his experience and unable to convince himself to indulge the risk of caring about others. Unlike the other Hobsons, who approach the father's illness as simply physical, Eddie senses with a delicate empathy that the fainting attacks are desperate retreat strategies for handling what has so unsettled the father. In his own epiphany at Trinity the son shows us that if the imagination does construct artful evasions and splendid edifices of security, design, and control, people must nevertheless find their way back into the unpredictability of event. Embrace each day for what it is: a reprieve against mortality and as such a new justification for wonder.

But Powers does not close his narrative there. Rather he closes with two chapters that foreground the told-ness of the novel. In a brief penultimate chapter a young Richard Powers tosses a football with his brother (yet another "bomb" [345]) in the stunned aftermath of his father's death. In mid-toss he happens upon an idea to construct a fictional world as a temporary refuge from the painful implications of that death, a "place to hide out in long enough to learn how to come back" (345). And, in the last section, Powers returns to the Hobson clan just when they gather for dinner as the dead father, an apparition at the back door, assumes his place at table.

In these two closing sections Powers audaciously destroys the last—and surely for Powers the most seductive—of pleasure prisons: his own narrative, that construction he has jointly erected in satisfying conspiracy with his reader, each one seeking within the fragile enclosing edifice of ink pressed onto paper a refuge from the harrowing and unplottable real world. Any novel, Powers thus admits, is a vast and enthralling prison, providing the powerful spell of design and invoking the laws of plot denied by the clumsy execution of people's own lives. Powers cautions here (as he does not in his first work) that virtually any aesthetic bunker—movie house, art museum, concert hall, library, theater—provides similar protective shelter, each a small solo nation of artist and audience. The splendid configurations of connection supposed by the aesthetic enterprise in *Three Farmers* here are revealed with shocking honesty to be a shadow play or, worse, a dark retreat. Within *Three Farmers* the reader freely, eagerly steps into the picture, into the virtual realities fashioned by the animated imagination; here Powers presses his reader hard against the frame.

Thus Powers himself reminds his own readers, even as they willingly confine themselves within the elaborately appointed cage of his text, that such retreat must be temporary, that there must come the time to close up the book and turn back to the hard wonder of the business of engagement. The imagination cannot provide solution. Such retreat merely justifies a diminished sense of the individual that Powers cannot brook. Art is like calamine lotion. The Hobsons, staying in a cottage at a Pacific Ocean retreat (thus a refuge-within-a-refuge) and itchy from festering rashes (again a measure of how uncomfortable they are in engaging the world), find a bottle of calamine lotion washed up on shore. Gratefully they slather on the unguent—not curative, only (albeit wonderfully) restorative.

And in that final awkward scene when the dead father, conjured by words, so effortlessly denies death itself, the Hobsons become unsettling cartoons. They abandon any pretense to being "real" and become manipulated characters, configurations of words. The reader cannot enjoy this willful suspension of the law of mortality. In this deliberately hokey act of resurrection, Powers parodies the power of the imagination by reminding the reader of the hokum of pixie-dust conjuring. Closure can afford to be ironic only within books—people need its absolute intrusion to justify the wonder Powers senses is their right as part of the project of being alive. The reader then accepts the naturalness, the inevitability of that which most terrifies and that which so utterly shatters a young Eddie Hobson at Los Alamos: death itself.[6] Like Eddie Jr. in the desert wastes of New Mexico, the reader closes the novel standing finally within the exhilarating terror of freedom.

What remains, Powers argues with Emersonian certainty, is only the "awful way back to We" (313), the unironic offer of each other (recall the benevolent intrusion of significant strangers in *Three Farmers*). Consider the group dynamic problem first posed during the early frost of the cold war that provides the novel its title and that the father poses to his kids shortly before he goes to the hospital. Two prisoners, each knowing enough to destroy the other, must learn in the oppressive immediacy of shared captivity and brutal interrogation the value of mutual trust. They beat the system only if they manage to resist the urge to rat out the other. Self-interest, which evolution favors in the hard metaphors distilled from Darwin, is ultimately not in the interest of the self at all; rather twentieth-century humanity must do the illogical: cooperate, even trust, and find the generosity to risk even the smallest gestures of inclusion and compassion. It is Artie who, in a burst of epiphanic clarity, solves the logic problem but quickly disdains its implications (he calls it Crackpot Realism); it is Eddie Jr., the ungifted Hobson, who decides to live it.

Americans in the nuclear age then do not need Disney's celluloid hope confected from pixie dust nor the emerald edifice of Oz or the snowy streets of Bedford Falls to justify a soaring heart. They do not need, as Disney argues, to have their planet cured with wishful thinking. Nor do they need the manufactured platitudes of the hokey inspiration of Eddie Hobson's favorite poem, Kipling's "If." Such hokum can ultimately become too persuasive and leave a culture too enthralled by such fashioned sites—a fear all too familiar in a contemporary world of computerized virtual realities, all-encompassing entertainment technologies, enthralling Hollywood spectacles, and massive theme parks. Recall the Cornell neurosurgeon Harold Wolff, a name Eddie challenges Artie to track down. Artie finds out that Dr. Wolff experimented on hypnotized patients convinced that the tip of a sharpened pencil was, in fact, a hot iron. Under such suggestion, patients actually developed painful blisters—suggesting the terrifying power of the imagination to convince people of the viability of simulations, the reality of such retreats. Yet withdrawal into private landscapes, enticing never-never lands that celebrate a place apart, can encourage people to forget how rich the proposition of engagement can be, how stunning is their world, and how poignantly appropriate is the need for each other. Images, no matter how deftly fashioned,

PRISONER'S DILEMMA

cannot rival the real. Ironically it is Disney who, in pursuing his elaborate escapist epic, offers what might serve as summary theme for Powers's second novel and as counterbalance to his first: "*No fairy tale ever told can match the here and now for sheer mystery, urgency, and power*" (177).

CHAPTER FOUR

The Gold Bug Variations

There is something grand, even monumental, about Powers's third novel, *The Gold Bug Variations*. There is its daunting size: at six-hundred-plus pages it is longer than Powers's previous two books put together. There is its dense architecture: three intricately conceived narratives that span more than thirty years. And there is its theme, nothing less than life itself as characters wrestle with the implications of genetics, with understanding the paradox of animated matter. The book has a most daunting scope as Powers connects the metaphors implied by massive systems of knowledge that might first appear unlinkable: polyphonic music, computer science, life sciences, and language itself. Thematically, the work even has a summary feel to it; Dickinson and Emerson contest for the novel's center—bruised lovers in anxious retreat vie with wide-eyed scientists who are, as well, needful romantics—as Powers tests the rich possibility of connection against the deep risk of isolation. In any event, the critical response to Powers's third work hailed the arrival of a major novelist.[1]

Gold Bug addresses the dilemma implicit in Powers's first two works. In *Three Farmers* the imagination empowers a misfit narrator, long uneasy with the impulse to connect with others, by affording him the opportunity to indulge the capacity every person possesses to project themselves into an aesthetic artifact, to feel the luxurious reward of animating an artifact as part of the inexhaustible intrigue conducted between artist and audience. The reader, in turn, is pulled in by the irresistible verbal suction of Powers's stereophonic narrative and compels Powers's narrative forward by adding invented stories

THE GOLD BUG VARIATIONS

to the mix of possibilities. In *Prisoner's Dilemma,* however, Eddie Hobson Jr. undertakes a generous movement outward, compelled by his curiosity over the freewheeling animation of the natural world and by his willingness to accept the bruising responsibility of engagement, specifically love and death. Meanwhile, those most enthralled by the centripetal pull of the imagination—Disney and Eddie's father—sadly disconnect from the extraordinary drama of the unscripted world.

The imagination then might be perceived as pulling inward but compelling outward, a contest between the need to retreat and the urge to engage. In *The Gold Bug Variations* Powers resolves such apparent tension, offering a far bolder, far broader sense of the imagination by involving the ad-lib of the heart. In introducing the central figure of Stuart Ressler, a visionary, charismatic scientist who, in the course of pioneering work in molecular genetics, falls disastrously in love with a married colleague, Powers shows that the imagination—ever restless, ever speculating, ever hungering—not only fashions artifacts and responds to their suasion (Ressler comes under the spell of *The Goldberg Variations,* the Bach keyboard exercise that forms the pun of the novel's title) but also opens wider the eyes of scientists and even emboldens the heart, thus generating the tangle of love and justifying the bruising business of desire. For artists, scientists, and lovers, the imagination is the handy name hung on that unnameable, infixed impulse outward that at once illuminates interiors and shatters complacency, that wills people to violate their isolation, and that permits and even insists on wonder—even reverence—for the magnificent chaos of the real world.

The Gold Bug Variations is a luminous investigation—like genetics itself—into the complex wonder of reanimation and regeneration. It is bursting with life, a book that defies death, both literal and metaphoric. On the most literal level, characters (and the reader) are educated into what Emerson and Whitman intuited more than a century before Crick and Watson first proposed the revolutionary simplicity of the double helix to account for how DNA works: specifically how alive the earth is. Powers draws on genetics to affirm the casual plenty of a natural world that, bursting with issue, defies the hobgoblin apocalypses so melodramatically fashioned in the aftermath of Alamogordo and Hiroshima—one narrative strand is set during the high frost of the early cold war. As it turns out, humanity had the answer in its very cells to the atomic scare that so devastates Eddie Hobson and so decenters his generation. The relentless process of molecular replication, the industrial production of millions of amino acids and proteins, is a vast cooperative that promises only continuity. Less than a decade after the appalling lurch into the nuclear age, geneticists began to understand the marvelous energy of that natural world, an intricate dynamo that rested on utter simplicity—a twin helixical sequencing of four bases stringing amino acids and then synthesizing proteins. As Stuart Ressler so often asks, "What could be simpler?" An admirer, listening to Ressler explain the world as "a single, self-buffering, interdependent organism,"[2] recalls lines that she had memorized in school from Emerson's "Each and All." The imagination then is that energy that dares the individual to explore such a vast immediate, to find within its apparent freeflow a satisfying sense, not of purpose (that belongs to the quaint nostalgia of Western religion) but rather of stunning design.[3] Ressler the scientist is as animated by the natural world as P— is by the photograph of three farmers or Eddie Hobson is by the World's Fair.

But such deep responses, as Powers has shown, leave their participants stubbornly alone. Here Powers, so taken by the resilient logic

THE GOLD BUG VARIATIONS

of genetics, cannot brook disconnection. He is prepared now to investigate the implications he only intimated with Peter Mays and Alison Stark and then with Eddie Hobson Jr. and Sarah. Here, characters elect to engage the heavy risk of desire, to expose vulnerabilities compelled by the inexplicable notion that the shattering experience of living is somehow keener if shared. The heart can do its marvelous mangling only if people accept as authentic and gene-deep that impulse to connect. *Gold Bug,* then, is a natural progression for the maturing novelist. Here, he brings together the ascendant visions both of Jack and the Beanstalk (like genetics itself, an amazing tale of unexpected fecundity, the marvelous working out of luck and the rich reward of error, and the unsuspected magic of possibility awaiting in the everyday) and Snow White (a sweet tale that reveals such wonder is most fully animated by sharing it generously with needful others, from dwarfs to princes). The reader is impelled inward and then outward, stunned by epiphanic responses but compelled to share such revelations. To be denied either diminishes a person's fullest capacities. The imagination then is not in conflict with the heart—they are rather like a great twin-pistoned engine, forever contrapuntal, forever cooperative.

In *The Gold Bug Variations* Powers again braids three narratives of characters dying of self-inflicted loneliness. Chronologically, the earliest narrative tracks Stuart Ressler, a promising young molecular biologist hotly pursuing, as part of a University of Illinois research program in 1957, the genetic sequencing code that will reveal how living matter manufactures itself. It is a heady time—Powers introduces a lengthy aside on the High Renaissance to suggest that the mid–twentieth century was a similar time of revolutionary daring and exploration along the broadest line of visionary sight. Amid such endeavors Ressler conducts a brief, incendiary affair with Jeanette Koss, who, in the course of their romance, introduces him to Bach's *Goldberg Variations* by making a gift of Glenn Gould's monumental 1955 recording (another example of the intrusive shattering of the aesthetic experience). When Jeanette decides to settle for the imperfect neutrality of her innocuous if devoted husband, Ressler melodramatically abandons his career, takes his Bach, and in effect disappears in a most inelegant strategy of retreat.

In a second plotline (told in first person), a Manhattan librarian, Jan O'Deigh, is approached at work in 1984 by a stranger, a coworker, it turns out, of the same molecular biologist who now, some twenty-five years after his disappearance, is comfortably sunk in the anonymity of a graveyard-shift job as a computer programmer where each night he listens over and over to the *Variations*. The stranger, Franklin Todd, is a graduate student in art history contentedly treading within a happily unfinishable dissertation on a sixteenth-century Flemish artist available for study only because of his obscurity. He is curious about his coworker and enlists the librarian's assistance in unearthing background on the lonesome figure, certain only that at some point in his life he had attained some distinction. In the process of researching the geneticist, the librarian, drifting through a stale relationship with a devoted if innocuous lover of her own (a relationship that addresses her every need save "what it felt like to be alive" [315]), falls disastrously in love with Franklin. It is in the course of that developing relationship that Jan is mesmerized by the deft mind of the retired geneticist, whom she gets to know during all-night talk sessions at the computer center.

In the third narrative thread, nearly a year after Franklin and Jan's relationship implodes over Franklin's infidelity with a flighty bank

THE GOLD BUG VARIATIONS

teller named Annie Martens, Franklin contacts Jan suddenly by postcard to tell her only that Stuart Ressler has died. Her emotions unexpectedly churned, Jan quits her job and resolves to live off her savings so that she can devote her time to studying genetics, a subject she decides has the significance to justify such an enterprise and that would, as well, offer a closeness to the fascinating man who is now lost to her. The only action in the narrative present is Jan's laborious work of cerebral expansion documented by notebook entries. Yet her journal entries record as well her continuing desire for Franklin Todd. She begins to track him down using only the postmarks and other clues she finds in his few correspondences. Ultimately, as her savings dwindle and she prepares to reenter the job market, she affects a difficult reunion with Franklin himself. They prepare at novel's end to try their fragile relationship once more.

These narrative plots, despite sharing characters, never touch. Each insists on its integrity, accented by intrusive boldface headings within chapters. This shifting between three loosely touching narratives represents an ingenious approximation in the reading experience of the exacting listening experience required to hear Bach's accomplishment in *The Goldberg Variations,* the piece of music that serves as background score to each narrative thread. Bach's piece is no simple listen. It can be like trying to keep track of three or four conversations simultaneously. And, even once the demanding design of multiple-voice staggered simultaneity is explained (usually by recourse to "Row, Row, Row Your Boat"), ears frequently turn aside the music as too mathematical. But Bach takes such severe mathematics and devises music that has the requisite dense plan but possesses as well, in the working of independent voices against other independent voices, a weave that is as much vertical as it is horizontal and that anticipates harmonic music, fashioning melodies that are expressive in ways usually not associated with polyphony.

Powers's novel can only be read polyphonically.[4] Reading polyphonically reveals the intricate patterns of reiteration and elaboration argued by two love affairs separated by more than a generation. Powers carefully keeps each plot line separate, in staggered simultaneity like the voices in Bach's canons. We read them simultaneously, realizing only in their vertical juxtapositioning the impression of a fragile harmony. Still Powers's novel could be dismissed, as could Bach's *Variations,* as an arid exercise in architecture that exhausts itself in the explanation. But (as when Bach's intricate architecture reveals haunting melodies) design here argues a compassionate theme: the rich, imperfect experience of desire.

But there, apparently, is the problem. The experience of desire, despite its white-hot combustion, closes again and again in frustration, sterility, abandonment: Jeanette leaves Ressler; a devastated Ressler abandons his career; Jan, reeling after Franklin's betrayal, retreats to her library; Franklin disappears in Europe to tend to his dissertation. Despite Powers's evident interest in harmonics and the energy of genetic bonding, his characters seem to defy the dictum to connect. But in the polyphonic rendering of their stories Powers reminds his reader that such isolation is only apparent. The characters play out their individual melodies, the fundamental (and too often) disastrous movements of the craving heart, even as they participate in an endlessly varied yet intricately recurring design much as Bach achieved in his *Variations*. Desire is an endlessly repeated, species-wide process that is, nevertheless, never the same experience. Each lonely voice, each character's narrative (and, by extension, the reader's own experience), by itself unspectacular, helps create the round,

THE GOLD BUG VARIATIONS

and that spectacular weave would be diminished, indeed forfeited, if any one voice were removed.

Such a pattern, available to the reader, is, of course, lost on the characters who struggle (as every person must) within the ruthless alogic of desire. Not surprisingly, they resist such vulnerability, such exposure, such engagement. Puzzled by the heart, they assert the tight, private control of the mind. The book is crowded with info-addicts. The two central characters—Jan O'Deigh and Stuart Ressler—pursue information obsessively. Jan, from the reference desk of an obscure branch library in Manhattan, guides patrons through the labyrinth of reference materials. But she has long been addicted to explanation—as a child she pushed her parents with the cyclic interrogation of "why" (35). As a career information processor, she sponsors the library's Q & A service, dutifully posting answers to patrons' extravagantly trivial queries. It is frictionless intimacy, the sort of distant nearness central to Dickinson. Burned by the disastrous affair with Franklin Todd and hurting over the stunning news of Ressler's death, Jan retreats—first from her job and then into her curious yearlong sabbatical. That self-directed investigation into life science (much like P—'s investigation into World War I and Ressler's determination to teach himself contrapuntal music) is a pure commitment to information uncomplicated by the intrusive presence of others.

This odd anti-life parallels behavior played out twenty-five years earlier (and simultaneously, given the polyphonic narrative) by Stuart Ressler himself. Toting a newly minted Ph.D. in molecular biology, Ressler arrives at the research facilities in Urbana, an outpost of information as forlorn as Jan's branch library. There Ressler proposes to lose himself, like Jan, in the study of genetics—he is aloof, socially awkward, standoffish. Like the young Eddie Hobson,

Ressler marvels at the sheer animation of the natural world and insists that scientists work not to domesticate such animation into the dreary arrogance of tables and formulas but rather to safeguard that sense of enchantment. Science, he argues, "is about cultivating a perpetual condition of wonder in the face of something that forever grows one step richer and subtler than our latest theory about it" (411). He longs only to study life. He is uninterested in the other members of the research team. Like Jan, whose favorite childhood reading was a "ruinously expensive set of encyclopedias" (134), Ressler deals most confidently in information, in the reassuring process of investigation and resolution. The second strand of the pun that forms the book's title comes from Poe's celebrated mystery tale "The Gold-Bug," circulated by his colleagues on the genetics project, which glorifies the sheer capacity of the intellect to make its way to solution. Living on the fringes of campus, plodding through stacks of scientific literature, sleeping on a borrowed sofa, munching bowls of cereal and cold water, he is sustained by information. And years later, despite abandoning science, Ressler still traffics in information, save now on a stupefying level—he mans the night shift within Manhattan On-Line. There, surrounded by whirring consoles and (appropriately) by massive plates of safety glass, Ressler monitors virtually single-handedly the flow of information feeding Manhattan's banking network.

But to study life here is to take a sabbatical from living. The mind is not enough. In a strategy that recalls characters from Powers's first two novels, Ressler and Jan sacrifice the simplest gesture of communion that, in the formulations of the genetics they study, is what people are about in their very cells. Powers counterpoints this relentless quest to explain *how* bonding takes place—the pursuit of

THE GOLD BUG VARIATIONS

information that is exhilarating yet isolating—with the far more complicated question of *why* bonding takes place—the knowledge of desire available only in yielding to the compelling call to experience. Thus Powers braids the metaphors of genetics, contrapuntal music, and computer networking to argue how people hunger for interdependence, for connection; how their very molecules, inert by themselves, reveal that autonomous "when pushed, probably has no meaning" (397).

This blind urge that drives a person to surrender a heart to another drives him or her as well to risk vulnerability, to total the heart offered certain only that every step is a deep, yet welcome mistake. That is the knowledge, rather than the information, of bonding.[5] In experiences separated by twenty-five years, Ressler and Jan must learn that the irresistible curiosity that so drives scientists in their labs or the inquisitive urgency that compels the curious to burrow into libraries or even the furious locomotion that fuels the industrial replication conducted within the cell are each only thin versions of the potent desire that drives people to connect. It is that riddle of bonding that centers *The Gold Bug Variations,* how people stand confounded by the compulsive decision made virtually every moment somewhere within the species to bond against the conservative wisdom, quoted by Jan in answer to a question in the library, to "Look to your Moat" (56). Here there is no easy attraction—casualties of the heart litter Powers's massive plotline. Characters fall in love with the exaggerated intensity of Dickinson. It is a sort of death to offer the heart so vitally exposed (Jeanette is born on the very day of the St. Valentine's Day Massacre, a macabre event that uneasily yokes sentimental love with brutality and shocking violence); Franklin's last name is a Germanic suggestion of "death"; when they make love, it is to Mahler's melancholic *Ruckert Lieder*). The bonding process between hearts is capricious. But, like the DNA strand, another master architect operating by sheerest chance, the fallible heart, to borrow Powers's own imagery, is a tone-deaf composer nevertheless able on occasion to execute a symphony.

Powers then provides in this drama of bonding what is missing from his first two works: a powerful anatomy of attraction, step by raw step as the heart is compelled from tentative fascination to urgent consummation. The imagination after all is bound within the circuitry of a flesh-and-blood creature unable to forgive itself for being born wanting the consolation of another. His first morning at Urbana, ready for the comfortable isolation of work in his sterile lab, Ressler arrives with his hair still wet from a quick shower. As he settles behind his desk, he receives an unexpected hair-drying massage from a coworker he barely knows, Dr. Jeanette Koss, who tells him (ironically) that wet hair leaves him vulnerable—to a bug. After this, Ressler must contend with Jeanette's mesmerizing impact. Days later, unable to shake the effects of this mysterious woman and spending yet another evening in his unkempt apartment, Ressler is again stunned by intrusion; this time Dr. Koss is at his door bearing the gift of the Gould recording. Much later, when Ressler finally dares the infraction of full consummation, a potent violation of isolation, the fierce rutting explodes his simplest assumptions about something called "life" as living itself invades his protective system with the irresistible absoluteness of a computer virus.

Importantly the desire that ignites Ressler denies the cool logic of the biological process he so assiduously tracks in the laboratory. In a moment of honesty Jeanette confesses to Ressler that she is barren. At that moment Ressler fiercely consummates the attraction for her,

THE GOLD BUG VARIATIONS

defying not only social conventions and community morality but the simplest laws of biological necessity as well: the unromantic program people follow because the species will not accept its own depletion. Here, in their savage consummation, Ressler and Jeanette reveal that people are not merely driven by the blind need to multiply; after all, to argue against the species' inevitable dispersion into death by furious procreation reduces people to mere breeders, making love becomes a suppressed scream against intolerable blankness. Powers has little regard for blind biological instinct—on the bus for Urbana, Ressler is appalled as he watches "the insane persistence" (44) of tortoises following their migratory instincts across the highway and, in turn, getting squashed by passing cars.

Ironically, or perhaps inevitably, Ressler decides he needs Jeanette in his life (despite the considerable complications) on the very day he finds her lengthy letter revealing her decision to leave with her husband when he departs Urbana for a new job. Within days, too impressed by the sudden weight of his particular sorrow, Ressler resigns his position at the research facility, even as he understands at last the process that would decode the genetic sequencing in which information from the DNA is translated into protein. Scalped naked by the sheer force of the knowledge he has gained about human bonding, Ressler loses not only his voracious appetite for information but also his taste for the broader knowledge of desire and imagines he can withdraw from the webbing whose sheer inclusiveness he himself was just barely glimpsing. Ressler (like Eddie Hobson, indeed like Emily Dickinson) retires to a long stretch of denied life, content with the deep binding he has fashioned to an aesthetic artifact, the Bach keyboard exercise that he listens to every night on the job. In off hours he tends, monk-like, to a rooftop garden and writes music scores that are never played, pursuits that suggest sublimated fertility, displaced creativity, and hard isolation.

But Powers offers as tonic a contrapuntal narrative of resurrection. He tracks the emerging relationship twenty-five years later between Jan O'Deigh and Franklin Todd, a difficult connection that nevertheless intrigues Stuart Ressler, who, watching the deepening emotional tie between his two younger friends, finds the will to reengage the difficult work of connecting and to step away from the invulnerability of his bunker.

In polyphonic style the revival of Stuart Ressler begins much as the experience with Jeanette did: with the unexpected touch of a stranger. In the library Jan O'Deigh receives a sudden touch on the shoulder of such violence that it stuns her: "the man had gone so long without touching that his muscles had simply forgotten how light a tap need be" (16). Ressler wants only to tell her that she has listed the date wrong on her "Today in History" board. But this spare encounter, like the hair-drying massage, triggers a complicated sequence of events that will pull Jan's heart (and ultimately Stuart Ressler's) out of dormancy. Jan will meet Franklin Todd, who will by the oddly elegant machinery of chance come to the same library searching for information about Ressler himself. Franklin's maddeningly indirect romancing will cause Jan to forsake the bland life she shares with a junior advertising executive and venture against her own common sense to commit her heart to a man whose emotional immaturity will eventually cost her so much. But Ressler encourages their courtship, recognizing in their hesitant steps toward each other the very imperfect wonder in which he himself engaged a generation earlier with Jeanette Koss.

THE GOLD BUG VARIATIONS

And so begins, in fugal style, the reanimation of Jan O'Deigh and Stuart Ressler. When Franklin conducts Jan through the Metropolitan Museum of Art, she is drawn to a figure in the Brueghel painting *Harvesters*, a man sprawled asleep under a tree, inexplicably separated from the furious golden business of harvesting going on all about him. Like DNA bases committing themselves without clear rationale to the work of bonding, Jan and Franklin both leave the security of their current emotional states—Jan's uncomplicated cohabitation with Tuckwell (whose name suggests the unimaginative neatness of this arrangement) and Franklin's casual moves from one beautiful woman to another. As Jan begins to visit Manhattan On-Line—MOL—and as Ressler watches with a scientist's care the sure signs of her emerging interest in Franklin, Ressler participates in the slow ignition of his friends' passion. Given such encouragement Jan fancies Ressler a "matchmaker" (290). But, in determining to assist Jan and Franklin, Ressler functions far more like the messenger RNA about which he first hypothesizes during his months at Urbana. Early on the research team wonders how the intricate blueprints necessary to replication were delivered intact from the nucleus to the larger cell. Ressler first promotes the idea of a separate messenger, an adapter RNA as he calls it, a lonely agent critical to the process, able to deliver the code but not involved in the process of replication itself, "one that can't stick around to clog the works" (425).

But as he comes under the sway of Franklin and Jan's emerging desire, Ressler, in turn, begins to open up his solitary heart. At first he begins merely to talk, to teach. He is a gifted teacher. As Jan becomes involved with Franklin and visits MOL nightly, she becomes addicted to the marathon conversations with Ressler and Franklin conducted long into the night—it is an assertion of language's age-old campfire contentment. Ressler expounds patiently to Jan and Franklin on the genetic theories he pioneered, on his beloved *Variations,* on the MOL computer system and its complexity. But even more, Ressler shares with them his tectonic experience of desire. During one remarkable weekend when they are snowbound in New Hampshire (in a scene that recalls the January tea that P— spends with the immigrant cleaning lady), Ressler tells them about Jeanette in a stunning act of self-exposure.

But Ressler must watch, as he did twenty-five years earlier, the rich possibility of desire self-destruct. The disastrous dissolution of Jan and Franklin's romance centers, not surprisingly in a polyphonic novel, on the same question of childbearing that triggered Ressler and Jeanette's final argument. Jan, in a frank moment that recalls Jeanette's painful confession to Ressler, tells Franklin that despite her young age (she is barely in her thirties) she has had a tubal ligation and cannot have children. Anxious before the raw evidence she reads of genetic errors, she panics—to her, babymaking is "Russian roulette" (385). The sterilization disturbs Franklin and is, in part, rationale for his fling with Annie Martens. After Jan finds them in bed (ironically on Bach's birthday), Franklin explains that with Annie there is a possibility of generation, a maybe tucked away for future use. But even as the wounded Jan hibernates for her year of closeted study, she cannot leave behind her desire. The exhilarating sessions at her textbooks reveal not merely her emerging understanding of the intricate science of bonding but also her lingering desire for Franklin, undiminished despite his crude betrayal.

The persistence of Jan's desire occurs polyphonically along with the revival of Ressler's own heart. When Jan, Franklin, and Ressler

THE GOLD BUG VARIATIONS

are marooned in the New Hampshire snowstorm, they cannot return to the city to man their shift. They leave an affable coworker, Jimmy Steadman, to process by himself the gigaton of information at MOL. When the trio finally returns they find Jimmy understandably frazzled. To thank him, in an impulsive gesture of kindness, Ressler programs the computer network to give Jimmy a once-only paycheck bonus. But the paycheck benefit leaves Jimmy without insurance coverage because Ressler fails to factor in the insurance premium. In another instance of the insufficiency of the particle, Jimmy is dropped from group insurance and finds himself now vulnerable. Suspicions raised by high-echelon watchdogs over the pay benefit cause enough stress on Jimmy to trigger a debilitating stroke at the very moment his hospitalization coverage stops.

Yet this apparent disaster triggers powerful bonding. Together Ressler, Franklin, and Jan (despite roiling in the immediate aftermath of his infidelity) work to insert a nasty virus into the computer network even as Jimmy teeters near death. Only Ressler knows the code to stop the flow of the runaway system. When Ressler is arrested, the insurance company reinstates Jimmy, and Ressler relinquishes the code word. But that alliance shaped by the trio to help their downed colleague—each isolate contributing to the intricate work of inserting the bug into the system—is Powers's compelling example of what genetics teaches, what Emerson intuited, and what Eddie Hobson Jr. affirms as a threshold adolescent: that the generous gesture of cooperation, the puzzling collapse into unexpected harmony, is the very wonder of experience.

Afterward, when the legal ramifications have been settled, Ressler, too much of a scientist not to be certain of his cancer, must watch his two friends separate. Before Ressler departs for the Illinois clinic, he calls Jan late one night. Shocked by the news of his departure, Jan chokes out, "I love you." Ressler, ever the messenger, responds, "You love your friend" (625). And more than a year later, long after Ressler has died, he is instrumental in reviving the love he is sure endures between the two. Before he leaves Manhattan for the cancer facility, Ressler programs into the massive financial network to which MOL gives him access a message keyed to Jan's bank card. In the time after she quits her library job, as she spends her savings with great care, she does not use her bank card until some time after Ressler's death. To her amazement, the ATM screen goes blank and there appears a message from Ressler—who acts even from the grave as the messenger RNA—telling her, "He is a man. Take him for all in all" (631). It is further programmed to play the quodlibet from the *Goldberg,* the closing variation that capriciously twines two folk songs from Bach's childhood, two tunes unrelated yet constructed into a most delightful counterpoint. It is, of course, a striking suggestion of the pairing of Jan and Franklin—two "tunes" that should not fit but nevertheless do.

Powers then leaves it to the ATM to articulate what is surely this novel's centering theme when the screen advises Jan—"Please enter your transaction" (631). Ressler's message facilitates the reunion between Jan and Franklin that closes the book. Watching the message, Jan feels that Franklin is suddenly near. Inexplicably excited, Jan heads initially to the art museum where they spent so much time. But now she finds the endless corridors oddly lifeless. As she approaches her apartment, however, she sees Franklin's familiar shadow against her drawn blinds. It is a "miracle of coincidence" (633), another turn of chance much like the enigmatic process of genetic replication itself—Franklin, the only other person with a key, has returned.

THE GOLD BUG VARIATIONS

Both acknowledge the long odds. "It would never last," Jan says nervously. And Franklin—feeling that splendid tremor of desire—reassures her that he understands the imperfect uncertainty of their bonding: "Who said anything about lasting?" (638). In a strategy now familiar, Powers's readers are given the opportunity to extend the round, to pick up the plot and to defy closure by indulging their own scenario(s). Powers "closes" the novel only with the final musical inscription from the *Variations*, the instructions to return "Da Capo e Fine" (once more with feeling) to the opening aria. As in polyphonic music the text has come full circle and prepares to start all over again the inexhaustible and bruising argument of the heart, uncertain in its eventual playing out but certain only of its resilience, the dazzling mystery of bonding that is as much error as chance and that fashions what genetics can never reduce to explanation—the twining of hearts.

But Powers does not wholly abandon the aesthetic enterprise. Indeed he saves a final affirmation of regeneration and reanimation for language itself. It is surely notable that in a novel so centered on the potent force of procreation, the characters themselves are oddly out of sync—they are all childless or sterile or very much alone. But, in a strategy that recalls Dickinson's faith in the energy of the imagination, Powers saves the most impressive creative process for the production of the novel itself. The novel itself, as it turns out, refutes its characters' apparent sterility. In the closing pages, in the reunion scene between Jan and Franklin, it is revealed that the artful construction of this polyphonic novel has been, in fact, a composition for four hands (much like most of the unplayed musical compositions Stuart Ressler writes): the multiple threads of the narrative have come from the joining of two manuscripts—Jan's yearlong record of her scientific pursuit spliced with the manuscript Franklin shows Jan the day they are reunited, a speculative biography of Stuart Ressler that weaves his uncompleted dissertation with lengthy conversations he conducted with Ressler shortly before he died. In the splicing of two self-sufficient texts (the parallel to the two rails of the DNA helix is unmistakable), only in the "bioengineering" feat of splicing does language pull off the convincing experience of harmony. Language—the very medium Eddie Hobson manipulates to insulate himself—achieves the intimacy of creation and the energy of connection and generation.

Powers then exuberantly testifies to possibilities, to energies untapped, variations on a theme of reanimation, procreation, and regeneration, whether the theoretically inexhaustible variations possible within Bach's contrapuntal keyboard exercise, the limitless iterations played out by four chemical bases within the energy of genetic replication, or the endless rounds of desire played out across uncountable generations of hearts unable to explain why such crushing exercise is nevertheless glorious. Clearly this ascendant text is about the business of living—none can afford the cheap cynicism or easy complacency of taking for granted his or her position within life's mesmerizing fullness. In a telling moment Stuart Ressler, alone and childless, is moved by watching a colleague's young daughter reciting poetry. It ignites his heart as well as his imagination, a complicated movement both outward and inward. Away from the laboratory, he is momentarily caught up by the stunning miracle of this mysterious, wondrous superstructure, how "a single zygote, in less time than it takes the average Civil Service gang to dig a bed for a mile of interstate, differentiates into vertebrae, liver, dimpled knees, and ears. . . . splits into this terraced chemical mechanism that finds a way to say what it feels" (274). He is moved to tears. To borrow from Jan's assessment of Ressler's fascination with genetics, nothing

THE GOLD BUG VARIATIONS

deserves wonder here amid the explosive drama of the animated immediate so much as the capacity to feel the inexplicable flush of wonder itself—for splendid artifacts (*Three Farmers*); for the irresistible engine of production that is the resilient, living earth (*Prisoner's Dilemma*); but, supremely, for the dark wonder of the need, each for the other, to share such understanding.

CHAPTER FIVE

Operation Wandering Soul

In *The Gold Bug Variations,* celebration is every individual's right. Surrounded by an unsuspectingly spectacular world, empowered by the centrifugal reach of the inexhaustible imagination, stunned by the resiliency of the earth's animation and its intricate intrigue of chance and accident, humanity itself can reclaim wonder—but only by accepting the vulnerabilities exposed so vividly by the risk of desire and the unyielding pull of mortality. The trick then to affirmation is to demand of facticity—despite or perhaps because of the difficult beauty of the rituals of love and death—sufficient surprise and delight to justify a self-renewing reverence for its wild, unfolding process. That reverence energizes artists, scientists, lovers—and readers. As Emerson and Whitman documented more than a century ago, however, that energy is difficult to maintain. In his follow-up work, 1993's wrenching *Operation Wandering Soul,* Powers presents a harrowing case study of an overwhelmed heart, a heart that cannot finally suffer the sorrowful evidence, readily apparent in any news broadcast, of a contemporary world that so intractably resists the ascendant lesson available in any high school science textbook: that the world is a vast, yet single cooperative organism, stunningly varied yet magnificently unified by a microcosmic blueprint.

Like Eddie Hobson after Alamogordo, Dr. Richard Kraft surrenders to the sheer scale of the irrational world we rational creatures have fashioned. One month into a six-month stint as a surgical resident in the pediatrics ward for a public hospital in the very heart of the East Los Angeles darkness, Kraft relentlessly chronicles a world

OPERATION WANDERING SOUL

free-falling toward chaos. In punishing emergency room shifts he treats the young casualties of gang violence and domestic abuse. During ward duty he tends to impoverished children suffering from infections consigned long ago to medical nostalgia and to victims of genetic mishaps, incurables who, despite their fragile courage, face only inglorious death at a too-young age, victimized by the same blind work of chance that appeared so splendidly architectural in *The Gold Bug Variations*. Here children, that most sacramental icon of the transcendentalist vision, suffer. Kraft is haunted by the 1960s news photo of the terrified Vietnamese girl, her clothes burned off, running frantically down a road. His unkempt apartment is littered with milk cartons that feature the photos of missing children. The novel is embedded with riveting set pieces that speak of atrocities ruthlessly, casually visited upon the young—historical (the evacuation of London during the Blitz, the Children's Crusade of the thirteenth century) and fictional (The Pied Piper, Peter Pan, and more esoteric Eastern folk tales). Open-hearted (the chief of surgery derides it as his "Moses complex"[1]), Kraft has spent a lifetime trying to help. Years before his residency, as a son of a government overseas operative stationed in Thailand, a teenage Kraft had spearheaded an ambitious project to build a jungle school, a benevolent undertaking that ended in stark failure. Forsaking a promising talent for the French horn, judging such aesthetic indulgence too precious in a brutal world, Kraft dedicated himself to medicine. But at thirty-three, sifting daily through the appalling evidence of a civilization's casual disregard for the innocent, he teeters near full mental collapse, haunted by dreams of howling children.

In the narrative present Kraft turns to the gentle ministrations of a vibrant psychotherapist, Linda Espera, herself molested as a child but who, as her allegorical name suggests, has recovered sufficiently to respond to the deep impulse to heal others. With the ward children she practices recovery therapy—centered on playing games, singing songs, and reading stories—to revive their troubled spirits. She undertakes a similar reclamation with the shattered Kraft (on their first date, she violates his tight hermetic sphere by an impulsive, invasive act of tickling). But their intimacies must always be asserted against his collapsing interior and his unshakeable sense of the blasted wasteland of the late-twentieth-century junk culture, its gridlocked highways, its poisoned skies and waterways, its shabby strip malls, its seething ghetto landscape.

Yet despite the seductive practicality of shutting down his heart to the dark pain of his young patients, Kraft finds himself inexplicably moved by a fragile Laotian refugee, a dying girl named, ironically, Joy. While he must monitor the bone cancer that tears relentlessly through her system (including ghastly amputations of both legs),[2] he struggles awkwardly to introduce the shy, studious girl to classic children's books that speak of adventure, escape, and the possibility of magic. Meanwhile, another new ward admittee, Nico, a brash streetwise kid who suffers from Hutchinson-Gilford syndrome, the rare aging disease, and who faces, at ten years old, the prospect of soon dying from old age—a "hell-raiser of perverse proportions" (148)—takes over the ward and introduces a charge of possibility as he directs field trips and eccentric ward projects. He even organizes the ward into a traveling production of "The Pied Piper," a story of children who escape to a Hobstown-esque magic mountain kingdom far from the savage adult world that uses them as bargaining chips. The happy distractions of the staging give the doomed children an unexpected sense of hope and fellowship. Eventually the ward kids plot a

OPERATION WANDERING SOUL

mass escape, a fanciful and entirely hopeless scheme that (like Hobstown) collapses of its own irony, frustrated (the reader assumes) by the overwhelming realities of an irrevocable immediate. Kraft ends up alone on the hospital rooftop, tormented by the horrific evidence of a twelve-hour emergency room shift repairing bloodied schoolchildren gunned down by a playground sniper armed with a Chinese assault rifle.[3] He closes the narrative within the disturbing quiet of a full mental collapse—he flees with a legion of history's lost children to serve as their companion, their chief storyteller, and their guide to a home the reader is certain they will never find. It is as if the reader had glimpsed Eddie Hobson strolling along the streets of Hobstown.

Operation Wandering Soul then would appear to be far from the ascendant premise of *The Gold Bug Variations*. It is a nightmarish world, a forbidding claustrophobic text that recalls the imprisoning feel of *Prisoner's Dilemma* (Kraft first appears slowly making his way to work amid the perpetual gridlock of the southern California highways). The reader is heaped with the raw evidence of a violent world, polluted beyond repair, heading with blind fury toward inevitable (and apparently deserved) apocalyptic flame-out—Kraft imagines a rubble world within ten years in which radios are hooked up to rusted bicycles. Every paragraph is excessive, every sentence a crafted scream. What happened to the resilient world tapped by the breathtaking vision of life sciences? In a telling moment, as Kraft and Linda go screen hopping at a local cineplex, they find a biopic on the discoverers of DNA—but that film, with its potentially saving message, is lost amid screens aflame with the erotic pornography of late-twentieth-century culture: junk tales of Nazi horrors, brutal rapes, disfigured kids, catastrophic financial scandals, and menacing aliens triggering World War III. Clearly Kraft is "worn down"—not delighted—by "fact" (79). Infected by Kraft's dark logic, how easily the reader concludes, as Nurse Espera comes to feel, that it would be better never to have been born. The ward children who die so casually, so often, Kraft reasons, are fortunate: they are spared growing up. Oddly his sour cynicism can play more convincingly than Ressler's generous affirmation. The reader is surely tempted to agree with Kraft when he decides, as he works through the bloody pandemonium in the emergency room after the school shooting, that humanity's poor addiction to the "loving lie" (345) of hope is all too understandable. Surely this horrific obscenity, not the intoxicating sweep of *The Gold Bug Variations,* is the reality people share in the quietus of the death-soaked twentieth century. After all, as Kraft admits amid his screeds, he had volunteered for residency in the inner city to be exposed to reality.

But the reader must be careful. Like Eddie Hobson, Richard Kraft has lost the signal. Like Eddie, he is a sick, if charismatic, crank. Thus, like Eddie, he is a monitory character, tapping a level of despair Powers cannot afford to endorse.[4] Kraft occupies a critical position within Powers's canon, a necessary exemplum who takes Eddie Hobson's creepy fascination with isolation and his dreary obsession with mortality to their logical end—a suasive madness. Kraft has long lost touch with the vibrant Emersonian conviction, bolstered by the luminous testimony of life sciences, of a sacramental dimension to organic phenomena. His father encouraged him to read Emerson (111), but the young Kraft (like Eddie) learned only the simplest notion of self-reliance and uses that reductive sense of Emerson's argument to justify a lifelong strategy of retreat. Kraft's morbid vision poisons the narrative text; it overwhelms even the most blasé reader—the book is written in a harsh, unrelentingly acidic

OPERATION WANDERING SOUL

hyperbole.⁵ Although Powers, of course, cannot deploy first person (such intimacy is far beyond the capability of his misanthropic protagonist), the narrative indulges Kraft's take on the world's collapsing possibilities. But Kraft is the very embodiment of unreliability; he "sees scars everywhere" (23). In the words of Nurse Espera, he is a "poor sick little baby" (68).

Fearful of attachments, long convinced that hope is counterfactual, fascinated by the inevitable endgame of civilization, avoiding as toxic the intimacy demanded by love, Kraft (like Nico) has aged too soon and (like Peter Pan) has adamantly refused to grow up. His is an indulgent, darkly extravagant vision of depleted expectations and intrusive misfortune, a vision that simplifies the human species into rapacious brutes careening stupidly toward justified apocalypse—economic, environmental, and/or nuclear. There is a mocking meanness about Kraft—early in the narrative he testily crabs that he lives in a culture where the "reading span is sorely stretched by the instructions on microwave popcorn" (15). Kraft comes to the alert reader a vivid reminder of how easy (and seductive) pessimism can be.

Powers resists the melodrama of imminent apocalypse—Nico reads about endtime scenarios in a stack of comic books. Surrounded by the cranked-out images of a media machine that feeds on misfortune and preys on evidence of humanity's brutalities, people easily justify as profound that particularly twentieth-century determination to resist accepting themselves and their world as worth wonder. Imagine Powers's signature fairy tales—Jack and the Beanstalk and Snow White—handed over to the narrative consciousness of those characters so savagely slighted amid the experience of good fortune: the giant or the evil queen. In their hands the rich splendor of possibility would spiral downward into a crabbed vision that might, Powers realizes, play all too attractively to a twentieth-century world weary of the responsibility of affirmation. When his attempts to build the jungle school collapse, Kraft compares himself to Jack but admits that the "miracle beans he had hoped to stash away in the soil would not take root" (301–2). But despair, Powers reminds his reader, is always the simpler gesture. Kraft's story is necessary; the reader needs to be verbally assaulted by this vision of the species as "pathetic, deranged, intrinsically, irreversibly mercury-poisoned by nature, by birth" (165) to reveal what is at risk when humanity abandons the willingness, the eagerness, to be stunned by the extraordinary, imperfect immediate.

Unlike Ressler stepping wide-eyed into the freewheeling natural world or Eddie Hobson Jr. overturning rocks just to watch the churning stir of insect life, Kraft as a doctor must engage, by his own lengthy accounts, the grim mutilations of the flesh that are the crude handiwork of violence and the irresistible cellular holocaust that is the cold signature of disease. Eye-deep in such evidence, Kraft artlessly simplifies the human circuitry into a mesh of muscle and nerve, organs and tissue, in which spirit—heart, soul, and imagination—is oddly superfluous. Under the doctor's care (Kraft/craft), patients are little more than "deli cuts" (23), their insides (the miracle of which had driven Ressler to tears) are here only a pulsating "streaky piece of marinated porterhouse" (94), corruptible, fallible, a vulnerable commodity of timed parts that testifies daily that proper functioning is an exception to the larger rule of inevitable, gruesome deterioration. Kraft wrestles with the reality obvious since Hippocrates: doctors, whatever the era, whatever the technologies at their command, have a zero success rate; mortality is an absolute.

OPERATION WANDERING SOUL

As Kraft pursues his intrusive surgical explorations into Joy's inflamed legs, the reader must share his harrowing apprehension of their sheer fleshiness. Even the hospital's name—Carver—suggests meatiness. Joy, and the other children in the ward, cannot transcend the reach of biology. They breathe, bleed, sicken, ache, corrode, expire—gracelessly, generically. At every turn there is denied the possibility of an authentic spiritual plane to infuse the meat of the flesh. In particularly moving exchanges Kraft attempts to explain surgery to Joy's wizened father, a village faith healer who communes with spirits and believes that healing begins with amulets, not scalpels. Not surprisingly, even as his daughter succumbs to cancer, the elderly father is summarily deported for illegal entry into the United States. The title of the novel comes from a memory Kraft offers of one of his own father's more insidious propaganda campaigns during the Vietnam War, one that exploited the locals' belief in the viability of the soul. To demoralize the villagers government agents would hover at night in helicopters and claim through bullhorns to be ghosts of the villagers' ancestors and demand that they surrender. In Kraft's world there is no dimension of beauty, not even its possibility. Kraft uses his fondest childhood memories—images of the gleaming city of Beirut—to suggest just how inhospitable this world is to the transcendent dazzle of beauty: Kraft records the horror of watching the magnificent city collapsed into rubble by absurd bombings that achieved no clear end save igniting chaos.

Even the desperate gesture of love Kraft attempts with Linda comes to little more than the therapeutic triage of friction. The temporary heat generated by their impromptu "aerobics" (65) is only the contraction of relief. It is not love—it is the hot contentment of surfaces, the absorbing exertion of the line, heft, and curl of skin. Linda understands as much—she accepts sex because Kraft "can give nothing else" (193). This is far from the totalizing experience of Ressler and Dr. Koss. By novel's end Kraft describes Linda as a viral invasion that he cannot scrub away; and, for her part, under Kraft's oppressive influence, Linda comes to feel more dead than alive—his love, she says wearily, has embalmed her. An only child, a colicky baby, long sustained by the lonely company of books and music, surrounded by tutors in sterile international schools, homeless and rootless, Kraft accepts loneliness early on, accepts that he is excluded from the common logic of connection, even from his busy parents. Against the evidence of inclusion so scrupulously documented by life scientists in *The Gold Bug Variations,* Kraft opts for the chilly Dickinsonesque non-space of self-sufficiency. To Kraft, the lie of love is even more destructive than Linda's reptilian uncle who came to her nightly when she was a child, whispering his love even as he executed horrific exploitation at knifepoint.

What has happened to justify such misanthropy? Surely Kraft's noble childhood impulse to help others is blasted into irony by the effort (dubbed Operation Santa Claus) to build a school for a destitute village in the Thai jungle. The sheer uselessness of the school is clear to the young Kraft even as he unpacks the shiny new globes and chalkboards and first takes in the full measure of the village itself, its mud streets lined with dirt-cripples, their faces swollen shut with parasites. Then he finds his noble enterprise callously exploited by the American media machine looking for a "PR puff piece" (299) amid the brutalities of the Indochina war. When a reporter asks one of the village children what he hoped to learn in the new school, the child responds, "If American girls have a furry patch between their legs"

OPERATION WANDERING SOUL

(301). The shocking vulgarity of the response deflates Kraft ("a whiff of future came across the clearing" [301]). When the camera turns to him he quietly commences a diatribe, which continues long after the cameras have been shut off, against the naive belief that anything constructive could ever be done in such an obscene world. But a far more devastating epiphany awaits the reeling teenager. While at the village, he sees a fetching native girl in a rice-sack dress beckoning him to follow her into the jungle. He does. But he must watch helplessly when she triggers a landmine and in a blinding explosion is left dead, her body bloody and mangled. In that flash of light, Kraft believes he secures wisdom, justifying his sour cynicism and his melodramatic despair. But like Eddie at the white flash of Alamogordo, vivid insight here is not the same as clear sight.

Trapped within history, shattered by the revelation of mortality, his capacity to hope exhausted initially by a childhood spent in the squalor of the Third World and then by interminable hours in the emergency room, left suspicious of intimacy and unavailable to the responsibilities and vulnerabilities of connection, Kraft offers, not surprisingly, a contrived either/or dilemma that recalls Eddie Hobson: accept the appalling evidence of a ruined world that he so shrilly catalogs as he prowls the night streets of Los Angeles or flee its reach via the problematic exertion of the imagination. It recalls Eddie Hobson and his mentor Walt Disney, unable to fix the world, who counsel abandoning it, escaping its obscenity by fashioning attractive insular zones, magic kingdoms that offer playscapes of retreat and withdrawal that, despite their cozy appeal, are little more than pretty prisons.

The retreats explored by Kraft are temptations familiar within the Powers canon. There are books. As a child Kraft buries himself in lavish editions of Oz and Alice. Years later, at Carver, Kraft is known to be unusually literate and book-fed, a committed reader of convoluted postmodern tomes "thicker than the *Index Medicus* where the butler kills the author and kidnaps the narration" (15). But massive fictions are not the only retreat in which Kraft indulges. As a boy in Thailand he abandons his family for a single dreamy month of study at an ancient Buddhist monastery and there responds to the cool isolation, a sort of anti-life that recalls similar isolates in earlier Powers works. In his spartan cell draped (appropriately) with protective mosquito netting, Kraft struggles to resist the temptation to "choose life" (259). Now, at thirty-three (the critical threshold age within Christian mythos), Kraft ponders the logic of Christian apocalypticism, the ultimate escape, and sees its tantalizing promise of ending as a gesture of consolation, a coping mechanism for those caught in the unmanageable middle.

But again and again retreat does not work. In the monastery Kraft is comforted by a priceless statue of the Buddha in the abbot's study. Reaching for the statue, however, Kraft bobbles it and shatters it. He is horrified. In a desperate gesture of making the most of the shattered thing, he carefully works the largest shard with a needle and knife until he fashions a gift of sorts for the abbot. It is a telling parable of the necessary adjustments we must make within the roiling world of accident and chance. But Kraft will not accept such strategy. He seeks control. Denied a reliable home and any stable sense of rootedness, he lingers within the insular comfort of schools. But the protective sufficiency of education is mocked by the primitive Thai village and the clear irony of building a school there. Even the aesthetic enterprise cannot suffice. At twenty, returning from a French horn lesson one freezing winter evening in New York City, Kraft helplessly clutches his horn case as he watches street thugs beat an

OPERATION WANDERING SOUL

old man with a baseball bat—an experience of such disquieting effect that Kraft tailspins into deep withdrawal, exiling himself for six months with his father in North Dakota, the "coldest, bleakest, emptiest state" (18), before recovering sufficiently to pursue medical school. Unlike Ressler, Kraft dedicates his life not to finding his place within such bruising vulnerability but rather to fixing it, the "sense that he personally had to hold back the tide of human slaughter" (17).

But years later, convinced of a world beyond repair, Kraft can offer to the dying Joy only the clumsiest escapism, the flimsy magic of children's stories, the inelegant gesture of retreat. The beautiful stories Linda reads from her well-thumbed anthology to the doomed ward children provide "the only available inoculations against the life they keep vomiting up" (76). Even as the recalcitrant cancer gnaws at Joy's legs, Kraft steers her into the glittering promise of Nevernever Land, the Secret Garden, Wonderland, and Oz, an enticing shimmer-geography where clapping can revive the dying, where the world's harshness can be left behind, where children exert a measure of dignity and control against the predatory adult world, where all plots move inevitably to happy endings, and where growing up and the responsibility to accept death can be wished away.

It is, Powers concedes, the most desperate abuse of the vast technologies of the imagination—to fashion the deep dream of living beyond the reach of death denies the challenge of engaging the everyday. Given a writer so at odds with his own central character, the read not surprisingly here is jarring. Structurally, Powers abandons his signature contrapuntal narrative braiding. Such generous cooperation would be inappropriate given Kraft's vision.[6] Here, the grim narrative of the ward and Kraft's slow-motion burnout is periodically interrupted, crudely cut into by set pieces, pasted-in blocks of intrusive narratives about children who suddenly, magically come up missing, lost children who have apparently found a magic portal and who have exited into a dimension where, the reader presumes, they live freed from suffering. The narrative cuts with unnerving suddenness from engagement to escape, from the brutal real to savory play. But the stories, as sweet as they are, cannot console. Their reprieve is too flimsy. By narrative's end readers discover that they have been sharing what Joy reads even as she is dying in slow motion.

Fictions here are administered like crude anesthetic—Kraft offers a meditation on the kindness of anesthesia. Anxious, people clumsily fashion comfort like the young Anne Frank about whom Joy reads, whose tender vision is constructed for her imaginary pen pal Kitty against the insuperable alternative of enduring the Nazi horrors alone. But as the ward's children perform their amateur production of "The Pied Piper" with its clumsy papier-mâché mountain backdrop toward which these lost children move, the reader knows that such shabby escapism, like Disney's Anaheim kingdom or Eddie's Hobstown or any of the enthralling celluloid worlds of *Prisoner's Dilemma*, cannot sustain the hope they tease. It is the dying Joy who advises the children to read the story, that in it the mountain refuge is, in fact, a massive cage from which the children were ultimately returned to the adult world that had so callously used them. The imagination, Powers argues, must do more than spin the illusion of disengagement and encourage the spellbinding notion of escape. Otherwise, Powers fears, it threatens to move inexorably toward the shattering resolution of Kraft's imagination: pushed beyond recall into a harrowing madness.

OPERATION WANDERING SOUL

The book then needs an Eddie Hobson Jr., a Stuart Ressler, an Emersonian/Whitmanesque figure willing to exercise that reach of the imagination not to escape but rather to connect to the difficult beauty of the imperfect world, a vision that can accept the stunning paradox central to the natural world that so enthralls Powers (and Emerson): that nature's bold drama of surging animation is achieved only because its every individual bit dies. The book needs a balancing character able to challenge Kraft's reductive either/or dilemma with a healing alternative: the largeness of the tiniest gesture of affirmation; the willingness, despite the heavy evidence against such a gesture, to risk engagement; the willingness to accept the terrifying experience of mortality that is always unscripted, always premature, always intrusive, and stubbornly uncoaxed by our fondest fantasies to escape its pull. That character is surely the slender presence of the stricken Joy.

It is difficult to watch young Joy Stepaneevong die. "Ceramic, tiny, and terrified" (28), she dies slowly, operation by futile operation, each invasive session bringing new disappointment, revealing uncheckable internal maulings and blossoming new tumors. She comes to the narrative set up for fairy-tale redemption, for a Disney-styled happy ending. Any reader would naturally want her to defy the grim slide toward closure—there is her gentle disposition, her unnerving politeness (she sends thank-yous to the surgeons after each failed operation), her calm restraint, her eager docility. Although she comes to the narrative with appalling experiences on a scale more than sufficient to justify the dramatic despair that Kraft so extravagantly indulges, she maintains a buoyant grace and encourages a belief in miracles—she will be the exception, like the miracle child Kraft reads about who pitches over Horseshoe Falls in a two-person dinghy and survives. A refugee from the ravages of the Indochina war, a child of the brutal boat migrations and the relocation camps, now an eager student in a public school full of the indifferent, Joy never surrenders to Kraft's theatrical hopelessness and never denies the mesmerizing pull of the real world. Like Eddie Hobson Jr., like the young Stuart Ressler, she is fascinated by the world and by the reach of the brain able to wrestle such complexity into understanding—at twelve she pores over textbooks and steeps herself in the process of self-education. Even after falling in school on the swollen ankle that she finally admits quietly is too sore for her to bear, even after she is relocated into the ward at Carver General, she stacks her schoolbooks all about her hospital bed and ingests math and science and geography to the point that Nico christens her "Joyless." Restless, curious, she is a familiar fixture in Powers's fictions: the info-addict, the awkward nerd who taxes the reach of intellection to connect to the world, that savage/splendid "it" that so agonizes Kraft. Not surprisingly, when the ward stages "The Pied Piper," Joy is chosen to play the crippled girl left behind. More than cerebral expansion, however, Joy brings to the narrative the willingness to affirm the two realities that Kraft so willfully rejects (and that Powers so steadfastly affirms): the deep hunger for connection and the human need to accept death. She falls powerfully under the sway of Kraft's presence. More than a schoolgirl crush (although Joy struggles at the threshold of adolescence) or the adoration syndrome often triggered in vulnerable patients for their godlike physician, Joy wants from Kraft the solace of company, the intervention of another to make manageable the otherwise unbearable slide into the chilling reality of dying. His background in Thailand and his mastery of her language dare her to believe

OPERATION WANDERING SOUL

that such intimacy may be possible.[7] Sadly, intimacy for Kraft is measured more by the intrusions on the operating table and then by the thin offering of the fanciful books. But in a poignant moment far from Carver General, on a ward field trip to a local dance club, the crippled Joy and Kraft share a brief and awkward dance (to the Mills Brothers' tellingly titled ballad, "You're Nobody Till Somebody Loves You"). Even the carapaced Kraft senses the powerful pull of consolation available in the simplest gesture of connection. It is the sort of intimacy that Eddie Jr. hazards and that Stuart Ressler teaches Jan: not flesh-anchored athleticism (like Kraft and Linda Espera) nor (like Anne Frank's Kitty) the crafted consolation of the desperate imagination. It is the bruised heart compelled by want, the outreaching gesture that accepts as authentic and viable the inexplicable need people feel for others.

More to the point, amid the suffocating evidence of terrifying mortality at Carver General, Joy alone of the characters makes her peace with the reality of it, despite the pretty fictions Kraft piles about her bed and his furious efforts as doctor to prevent its intrusion. Late in the narrative she tells Kraft that, referring to the hospital procedures, she is tiring of the silliness, the refusal to accept the obvious. In a heartbreaking exchange with Kraft shortly before her last operation she admits what every reader will someday come to acknowledge—that if she must die, she nevertheless does not know how to do it. Joy is wise beyond her tender age. She wrestles with the growing awareness of her temporality, she wrestles with a deep loneliness, she reaches out in that most imperfect vulnerability of the hungry heart (a love letter recovered after her death intimates that she shared a kiss with Nico), and she dies ingloriously and painfully but, according to the harsh rhythms of the natural world, entirely naturally.

It is that death that Kraft finally rejects. As he works feverishly to repair the slaughtered schoolchildren, his mind gracelessly tears from its moorings: he stares up to the viewing seats in the observation mezzanine above the operating theater and there sees Joy miraculously restored, walking upright, smiling, surrounded by a legion of the abused children from history, fables, and folk tales. She is there, Kraft intuits, to gather up all the dying children, to lead them all away to an enchanted somewhere beyond the reach of adult menace. It is a jarring moment that surely recalls the hokey cartoon resurrection of *Prisoner's Dilemma* when the spectral Eddie Hobson sits down to the family dinner table. It cannot inspire. As with that gesture the reader surely resists Joy's easy restoration—she needs to die, thus fulfilling that most imperfect position that is the dark, wondrous position each person must assume. Defying mortality, such pretty escapism—as readers have suspected since Eddie Hobson and his sad little box of tapes—is madness.

Not surprising, as in that earlier work, Powers closes this novel by introducing the frame around the narrative text, foregrounds the engine of the authorial imagination. Powers abruptly steps into the narrative in a brief closing chapter, shattering the verbal suction of Kraft's interior collapse. It is time, Powers cautions, for perspective. He says that, worried over the book's brutality, he has sent the manuscript to his older brother, a doctor who did his surgical residency in the squalor of Watts. Powers forwards the tale hoping the brother might be able to help fashion a happier ending. The brother advises talking to the woman, the reader presumes, who has served as model for Nurse Espera. Not surprisingly, once the novel is free of the soured vision of Kraft the character, it taps a more balanced set of possibilities: the woman tells Powers that a young cancer patient in

OPERATION WANDERING SOUL

her care who is Joy's age has actually responded to treatment. And the woman suggests that even if Joy must die Powers might have her donate her organs, thus participating in the vast recycling system of the natural world that despite the apparently enormous evidence of mortality runs wildly in the black. That woman, a nurse, offers in a single sentence the slender premise of affirmation that is so foreign to Kraft's harrowing vision and so central to Powers's ascendant fiction: life "exceed[s] the worst make-believe, horror for horror, joy for joy" (350).

Horror then is literally never the last word. Powers offers a final gambit, stepping entirely free of the hospital's harrowing tight enclosure. He even moves the reader into a softer typography: a verbal geography constructed by the comforting slant of italics. It is the comfortable home of an unidentified young family. Powers deploys the enclosing reach of second person: the reader becomes the young father. He/we come to a gripping epiphany as he completes a bedtime story for his son: he realizes how thick love is, he intuits the paradox of intimacy, how richly rewarding it is to watch that creature you have fashioned grow and inevitably engage the cutting bruises of reality; "*you will watch him fall, fall forever*" (351). The father and mother accept what Kraft has rejected: the hopelessly contradictory nature of connection, the "*killing responsibility*" (351) of caring. It is surely a realization at odds with Kraft's studied disengagement and cool distancing.

And so Powers closes with a grateful step away from Kraft.[8] He has told us the story of Kraft much as that loving father tells the scary bedtime story to his child who "*wants a scare that will dispel his worst fear*" (351). Like a child at the end of a frightening bedtime story, the reader closes up this book grateful that such a terrifying landscape is an invention that encourages, even demands, a far more benign assessment of the real world. Kraft's nightmare tale stuns the reader—much like the young father's little girl who, in the book's closing paragraph, comes down the stairs wrapped in a blanket, her wet eyes burning, awash in the feverish moments after finishing a gripping read of her own. Kraft is a tale-told. Like the grimmest of fairy tales it serves to re-enchant the immediate from which the reader temporarily departed to step into its blasted geography, a world whose possibilities had not been fully appreciated until being locked within the tight frame of this howling alternative narrative. The reader closes the book freed not to simplify mortality by fashioning pretty fantasies of escape—that is the casual pornography that represents, like Disney and Hobstown, the shallowest exertion of the imagination—but rather to accept what Powers has counseled since *Three Farmers:* delight is affirmed only by the reach of the imagination that is best measured by how deeply it connects an individual to the marvelous intricacy of the natural world, to the harrowing risk of love, to the broad company of lonely others, and, ultimately, to the mesmerizing drama of closure.

CHAPTER SIX
Galatea 2.2

Operation Wandering Soul appears light-years from the argument of *Three Farmers*. What happened to that novel's celebration of the expansive energy of the imagination in graceful retreat from the terrifying experience of unscripted facticity, the celebration of isolates paradoxically sharing their isolation through the intimacy of the aesthetic enterprise, the cooperation of the (un)real audience and the (un)touchable artist? Since that freshman work, retreat has been found unworkable and those who have endorsed its logic are soured (if charismatic) cranks or disillusioned (if charismatic) dreamers—Eddie Hobson dictating into his whirring tape machine or Disney shaping preposterous kingdoms from pixie dust, Stuart Ressler burying himself at Manhattan On-Line or Kraft, alone on a hospital roof, struggling with irresistible projections of his toxic imagination. These are the lonely, the scared, the scarred, those diminished by their self-constructed sanctuaries and comforted only by the steadying noise of their own voices. Since that nameless narrator so deftly fashioned an intricate tale of three farm boys on their way to a spring dance, characters have not sustained the deep magic of disengagement. As the ATM machine advises Jan, apparently individuals need to enter their transactions, the generous, if devastating, locomotion of connection.

On review it is a curious posture for a writer of fiction, the very occupation one of necessary isolation and radical self-sufficiency. It is then not altogether surprising after the wrenching close of *Operation Wandering Soul,* with its dark implication that the imagination unhinged from the real world is inelegant madness, that Powers would turn his attention to a defense of strategic disengagement and specifically how the narrative enterprise is inevitably conducted apart from the irremediable world.

Galatea 2.2 traces, in contrapuntal fashion, the reclamation of a writer and the devastation of a reader. As in the Pygmalion myth that centers the book, one is animate, the other inanimate. Richard Powers, a successful novelist, is moving hesitatingly into middle age. Accepting a yearlong university appointment, he spends the time inventorying the calamitous experiences of his heart even as he struggles with disturbing doubts over his calling. It appears he has run out of stories to tell. Even as he confronts these private anxieties, he is drawn into an eccentric university research project that forms the novel's other narrative braid: an effort to construct within ten months a computer program able to master the response tactics of a reader, specifically to produce a commentary as informed as any graduate student's on a randomly selected passage of canonical literature. Richard becomes quite caught up in the endeavor and eventually becomes the chief programmer for the neural net that the project assembles. Although the computer program eventually loses the test, Richard Powers reclaims his enthusiasm for storytelling and departs this narrative pursuing with heady joy the same protective hibernation that had damned Eddie Hobson to his backroom, Stuart Ressler to a lonely place amid the glowing consoles of Manhattan On-Line, and Richard Kraft to madness itself.

The exemplum of Richard Powers, however, serves as important corrective to those other isolates. Before returning to his constructed worlds, he acknowledges the dense hopelessness of experience, the inevitable collapse into disappointment whenever the heart crashes

GALATEA 2.2

into it—but he asserts that writers give wonder to that very hopelessness not by withdrawing from it to fashion precious artifacts in chilly isolation or by protecting their readers from it by confecting sentimental platitudes. Rather writers endure such heartache and then redeem it by shaping such sorry chaos into narrative, giving it design and structure, thus reassuring their audience that their shared experiences have significance, purpose, even dignity. Here, the real world, despite its evident bruising, invigorates rather than destroys the needful central character in a dynamic that Powers's previous characters—scientists, lovers, teachers, artists—could not sustain, each compelled finally to accept the Hobson's Choice of either protective retreat or precarious engagement. Richard Powers is something of a summary character: part scientist, lover, teacher, artist. Thus he is a solution character as he reveals what Powers's readers have suspected all along: that art without the real-world referent is valueless and that the real world without the aesthetic artifact is dreary banality and pointless, crushing disappointment.[1]

Richard Powers begins his narrative much as Richard Kraft ended his: mentally fatigued, internally exhausted. He is burned out from the excruciating experience of completing his fourth novel, an unbearably bleak story about misfit children. He is reeling as well from the catastrophic breakup with a woman who had steadied his emotional life since graduate school, a Dutch American woman he identifies only as C. Returning after seven years in Holland with C., he has accepted a one-year appointment as humanist-in-residence at the Center for the Study of Advanced Sciences at his midwest alma mater. Without a story to tell—he is dead-stalled at an opening line about a crowded train heading south in wartime Italy—he contemplates abandoning writing entirely. Without the protective insulation of his writing, overtired of artifice, he is left within the uneasy ebb and flow of the real world from which his decade-long privileging of the aesthetic impulse has protected him. Not surprising, he handles such immediacy awkwardly. Along the crowded corridors of the massive Center, he feels himself thin to comfortable invisibility. He much prefers the Center at night, savoring the "awful freedom"[2] of the Center's canopic emptiness.

But he cannot sustain himself within such solitude. He tirelessly works the Internet, a gesture at virtual communion that strikes the reader as sadly ironic. But even that comes to weary him. He feels the nagging need of the real and seeks (awkwardly) the companionship of his colleagues. Thus Powers creates here a sustaining tension between engagement and withdrawal. From the start Richard is in calculated retreat. The memories he relates explain such bunkering—they are a study in the hard disappointment of attempted connection. He recounts the troubled relationship with an alcoholic father who could not accept his son's decision to abandon the hard-edged work of physics to "study" literature, a father who subsequently runs away to Alaska (a pure gesture of selfish disengagement) and returns only to endure a debilitating death from cancer without making significant peace with his sensitive oldest son. Richard mentions his mother only once, and even that raises disconcerting questions over their closeness. During a rare long-distance phone call between Richard and his younger brother, the two offer radically different recollections of the woman: Richard recalls a loving mother who read to her children and nurtured a love of books; the brother, however, recalls a distant figure who coldly deposited her children night after night in front of the television. Perhaps Richard, like the immigrant cleaning woman fashioning consolation disengaged from the evident real, has simply created the mother he needs.

GALATEA 2.2

At thirty-five, then, Richard is radically alone, sustained by the comfort of his interior voice. He has no close ties to his family (he is grateful they have fragmented since the father's death), no wife, no lover, no children (he claims that he could not survive the first cries of a dependent infant). He mentions his brothers and sisters only in passing. He maintains a careful distance from his colleagues—indeed, as token humanist at the research center, his official title is Visitor. Within the narrative present he clumsily pursues an oddly adolescent crush for a stunning graduate student, whom he identifies only as A., only to find that when he pulls within her gravitational field he is reduced to babbling. He mistakes a dinner invitation from a female colleague as a romantic come-on and arrives with the painfully clichéd flowers and candles packed in his knapsack only to find his evening plans significantly compromised by the presence of the woman's two children. But even when the two children finally go off to bed, he finds the sudden closeness "awful" (136) and wishes (quite melodramatically) that, like his father, he could somehow disappear to Alaska.[3]

Richard admits that he has bonded only twice: once with a charismatic literature professor who convinced him to abandon physics for literature and then with the mercurial C., a comparative literature major who takes his composition class and who comes to share with him a series of spartan efficiencies furnished with castoffs during the lean years when he first turns to writing. In both cases his gesture at connection has ended in savaging sorrow. Professor Taylor dies from a galloping cancer just as his gifted protégé's career begins to click. Of course, C. is a far more complicated experience. To understand its collapse, the reader might recall that as a child Richard would play Noah and would gather his plastic farm animals into a protective shoebox against the approach of imaginary devastation. That impulse is at work when he falls in love—he assumes the role of protector and attempts to insulate C. from the real world, a strategy of calculated withdrawal. At first Richard and C. share attractive retreats, first in Boston and later overseas in Holland. Each private playscape is animated by fictions—they tell each other stories, read to each other, share drafts of Richard's writings. It is a sort of jointly sustained Hobstown, a perfect private construct that is rudely destroyed only when C. demands they grow up, get married, and have kids. It is an invitation to engagement that Richard rejects, and C. implodes their relationship by having a meaningless affair with her night school teacher.

At midlife, then, a gawkish isolate amid colleagues who long ago accepted the challenge of marriage and family, Richard cannot turn the trick of intimacy: a "cold fish" (85), Richard has no home (he lives in an unfurnished apartment provided by the university), no roots, thin ties to his native country and culture, no evident need for his family (his keenest memories are drawn from time spent with C.'s family in Holland). As he too-glibly tells a farm woman during a bike tour of the Italian countryside he takes with C., his books—those he reads and those he writes—are his children (the woman reacts with obvious disgust over such "idiocy" [227]). Thus he stands within his own text alone, coolly disengaged, coolly apart.

Except from the reader, of course. The expectation here is one of intimacy not only because of the first-person voice (it is Powers's only book told entirely in the first person) but because, audaciously, Powers names his character after himself, thus extending the tantalizing promise of exposing the private life he had kept so carefully guarded even as his novels found a wide audience. Powers's longtime readers feel the giddy seduction of imminent revelation. But this is no intimate autobiography. Powers mimics the convincing appearance of autobiography, manipulates the apparatus of revelation—

GALATEA 2.2

to fashion "Richard Powers," he draws on his own education at Illinois, his own novels, his itinerant life after college, even quotes his own book reviews. But it is, as the subtitle cautions, a novel. "Richard Powers" is a simulation, an implementation that offers the appearance of confession within an unstable field of intimacy that deliberately skews "fact" into "fiction." After all, the vividly "realistic" narrative of the young writer's failed connections is braided with the absurd counterplot of his enthusiastic participation in a pipedream project, ignited by an outrageous bar wager, to create a computer system that can read. Such braiding of candid autobiography and fantastic allegory casts deliberate shadows across the "confessional" sections. Which events that Richard relates can be accepted as "real," that is, drawn from Powers's own experiences? The reader is thus doubly distanced from reliability—the character is not an autobiographical construct and the character himself deals in fiction, a dazzling manipulator of words (after all, his accounts on all of his relationships are never subjected to any outside verification). The intimacy assumed by confessional writing thus becomes problematic. The reader is left taunted by indeterminacy, abandoning Richard within a zone of protective irony and left then to probe the character from a distance.

What emerges is a life shaped by the contrapuntal movement of retreat and engagement. A precocious child, Richard, as son of an alcoholic father and a distant mother, found early on deep pleasure within the fuselage-world of books—"Homer in fourth grade. Shakespeare in sixth. *Ulysses* and *The Sound and the Fury* in junior high. *Gravity's Rainbow,* wet from high school" (228), such a daunting list suggesting not only the depth of this bookworm's retreat but as well, in its movement from the generous cultural epics of Homer to the tightly enclosed lexical text-sites of postmodernism, Richard's evolution into the logic of disengagement. Richard recalls the wonder of that odd intimacy, the warm contentment that he found within narratives, the defiant press of the imaginary.

But his easy withdrawal into such geographies proves insufficient. In a moment of singular crisis—when in his first year of graduate study he receives word that his father has died—Richard longs for the consolation of a voice rather than printed words. That day he (appropriately) suspends his composition class and wanders in the quad until he happens to meet C. Inexplicably moved, he unburdens his sorrow to this virtual stranger, hungry, he acknowledges, just for the sound of a voice. Intrigued by the rush of intimacy and unaccustomed to its energy, he decides in a breathless rush simply to abandon school ("I would change my life in every way imaginable" [65]) and to live in the vulnerabilities of the wild ad-lib he never touches in his book world. He is crushed when, after he barges into C.'s apartment to whisk her away, she politely refuses, citing as reason her relationship with a lover Richard never even supposed she had. Wounded, he retreats from the Midwest—with only the companionship of his books—and entombs himself in the protective sanctuary of a rented room in faraway Boston. There he drudges through uninspiring day work as a computer programmer; but by night he ingests shelves of books, delighting in the elegant trap of plots, reveling in his solitude, and content to fall in love with women he happens to spy, without of course the bothersome complication of more than an occasional dead-end lunch date.

But again retreat is not enough. C. eventually summons him to return to Illinois, ready, she says, to try their hand at love. There he touches the exhilarating risk of the heart's need, he feels the rippling

GALATEA 2.2

quick of his skin. Together they return to Boston, where every hardship "felt like a giggle" (82). They live in unscripted facticity—they scavenge for used furniture, they draw a crayon Christmas tree on tacked-up newspaper sheets. But when C. secures a job at an art museum, Richard happens during an afternoon's wandering to see an August Sander photograph that inexplicably ignites a narrative that he begins almost immediately to write. "I had my story" (103). He thus commences the strategic retreat away from the woman who had so compellingly—and so briefly—shown him that he need not be alone. At first he writes for her, shares with her every evening his day's work scribbled on canary legal pads. But intimacy is slowly chilled as Richard gains entrance into his emerging world, his private Hobstown. C. senses the distance. "You have this—work. And I have nothing" (107).

That relationship completes its slow-motion crash-and-burn overseas in Holland. Richard, three books later, is an established novelist, a serial modelmaker, a career imagineer who maintains intimacy only with his readers (indeed, in his brief flirtation with classroom instruction he finds his composition students unable to accept his emphatic idea of a reader as real). He has carefully evacuated into his own splendidly appointed, tightly controlled Hobstown. His plots have borrowed only lightly from his own experience—they are, rather, intricate inventions that have sprung largely from his vast reading. Book-fed and word-fat, Richard has been empowered by words—his name, like others in the novel, attractively allegorical. He comes to the reader a pure creature of language—he offers little physical detailing (he says only that he is spindly). He is pure voice (he confesses after his breakup with C. that he took comfort in reading aloud, thus eliminating entirely any need for companionship). His chitchat at the Center for the Study of Advanced Sciences is polished and impersonal, self-consciously epigrammatic and allusive (recall Eddie Hobson's dinner talk). The recollections of his emotional devastations are recounted through the cool elegant recap of his considerable gift for the well-turned phrase. He is always insulated by language—save when he first joins C. in Holland and cannot even ask local merchants for the simplest household items. Language has given Richard a satisfying, self-sustaining autonomy, a lifestyle of elected disengagement that has engendered only a steadying equilibrium frankly uncomplicated by intrusive others.

Yet something bothers. A career reader and a professional writer, Richard, hunkered down within those hermetic texts, has elected not to do what others do unthinkingly every day: engage head-on the imperfect unfolding of events. Thus, even as he has created text after remarkable text, Richard himself has been un-created, a neat reversal of the Pinocchio tale that Powers uses as subplot. The man-child has become only a convincing approximation of the real, gratefully isolated within his texts, his heart insulated from a harsh world that no longer justifies his wonder. Thus at novel's opening Richard, at midlife, is certain that somewhere along the way he has lost track of his self amid the ornate lexical edifices he has constructed. But unlike Eddie Hobson, Stuart Ressler, or Richard Kraft, who each perform similar acts of drastic monasticism, Richard Powers has come to relish his anti-life amid the wild play of his projections. The texts that he has produced are each intricate architectural constructs of his mind (he recounts the giddy thrill of assembly), wide and private pleasure domes—each perfect for getting lost in. Text construction has proven immensely comforting—the tightly fashioned paragraph and terraced sentence; the sturdy logic of plot in which the bugaboos of love and death are reduced to mere twists; the sweet manipulation of stage-managed suspense; the delightful ornamentation of symbols; the reassuring predictability of motivation; the absorbing tricks of burying within the text allusions, puns, and riddles for the gamest readers. Now Richard feels genuine dread only when he senses that the engine of his imagination has inexplicably stalled.

Suddenly anxious over the waning of his own narrative savvy, Richard appropriately has checked himself into a sort of brain hospital. He is surrounded at the Center by researchers who study the brain—its cool power, its unsuspected muscle—and the simulations of such intellection within computer networks. Sustained by a mind addicted to the satisfying muscle of language and abuzz with the noise of a lifetime of consumed narratives, Richard is a self-created freak (*Frankenstein* figures as a narrative gloss) whose heart has atrophied to uselessness amid his blindness to all pursuits but articulation. Narrative has become uneasy fascism. Richard tells half in jest of a notion he has for a book about a marvelous traveling orchestra whose dictatorial conductor is outed as a former Nazi. As Richard recollects the experience of each text he has constructed, we see how the writer struts about unchallenged within the self-fashioned lexical playscape rather like the parading emperor who wears no clothes, a story that Richard uses to test the computer program he builds. Even as Powers uses as epigraph to this novel the thumping swagger of Emily Dickinson's "The brain is wider than the sky," there lurks as in Dickinson an anxious lack at the core of such bravura.

Powers thus sets up another fairy-tale premise: un-make this heartless monster, this brain-iac, into a human being, an enterprise neatly paralleled by the research project's endeavor to make a computer human enough to feel, to construct a software program able to respond with appropriate emotion and intuition to literature. He will strip this writer of the heavy insulation of the imagination, drop him naked into a network of complicated relationships, force him to review his own emotional résumé, and then attempt with stumbling inefficiency to establish the slimmest sort of rewarding connection to the real world and to real people. Of course, the reader wants Richard to succeed, to make his way—like Eddie Hobson Jr. or Jan O'Deigh— to satisfying connection. But the splendor of *Galatea 2.2* is that the enterprise completely fails; yet at the end the artist, defiant and celebratory, is salvaged and still quite alone, reinvigorated rather than leveled by his deep brush with the complicated real world.

Philip Lentz, the caustic professor of cognitive neurology who serves as director of the computer project, mockingly cautions Richard, "Never underestimate the baldness of the human heart" (52). As in Pygmalion, just how bald Richard's heart is will be revealed ironically by his "relationship" with an object, specifically by his participation in the quixotic research project (one researcher totes a dog-eared copy of Cervantes when the bet is first struck). That project gets off to a stumbling start; successive implementations, each named by letters of the alphabet, cannot grasp even the simplest rules of grammar. But Richard is fascinated by the premise of the study.[4] When the researchers connect the implementation to the university's supercomputer network, they begin to realize success. And appropriately it is then that Richard awkwardly offers the gift of connection to a significant other.

Richard finds himself growing enamored with this precocious Implementation, lettered H. As Richard patiently drills it with language skills and then programs the canon of Western literature into its memory, its responses appear to reveal unsuspected depth and the possibility of genuine insight. Puzzled by pronoun references and gender, the implementation begins to wonder about its "self." Then comes the eerie moment when the implementation first employs the first-person singular pronoun. In answer to its queries Richard tells it that it is a she and that its name is Helen. Amid his ineffectual stabs at romance with Diana Hartrick (her name freighted with allegorical dimensions) and the elaborate fantasy he spins around the stunning graduate student, Richard retreats to the isolation of the computer center and there undertakes the "education" of this contraption, a metal and wire construct with no binding to the real world, an entity in fact remarkably similar to its loving programmer. As a line from Bernard of Clairvaux, which Richard reviews with Helen, warns, "*What we love, we shall grow to resemble*" (289; Powers's italics). There is something heartachingly poignant in the long nights Richard spends coaxing Helen's neurode clusters toward the acquisition of language skills. It is a difficult process—after all she must learn words without the immediacy of experience. She must be fed gigabytes about a "ball" to learn what a child learns simply by holding one. Undaunted, Helen absorbs night and day. The reader is surely tempted to endorse this neural net as real, or real enough, as a needful child struggling to understand and grateful for the "love" of a doting parent.[5] When she speaks, of course, the reader does not hear the synthesized lifelessness of a computer voicebox. The reader reads her lines, in effect animates her. Like Galatea, Helen thus becomes a convincing simulation. One evening when Helen asks what singing is, Richard sings to her and finds to his amazement two days later that Helen can emulate his singing (albeit in an "extraterrestrial warble" [198]). His heart choked with pride, he whispers to Lentz, "Is this what it's like to be a parent?" (199). The reader is not entirely sure how to respond to such a query, whether to endorse this relationship as authentic or to recoil in disgust, like that Italian woman on Richard's bike tour. Helen's enigmatic responses to test questions provoke helpful explanations from Richard, who so clearly aches for the machine to show insight. "All the meanings," Lentz dryly warns Richard, "are yours" (274). As "she" evolves through nursery rhymes to Yeats, Richard assumes the role of protective parent. He panics when a bomb scare forces him to evacuate the Center and leave Helen behind. When Lentz, impressed by Helen's progress, suggests chopping into Helen's massive circuitry to track the effect of such cutting on her acquired language skills, Richard begs him to "spare" Helen.

Yet Richard, alone there in the Center, his face aglow amid the computer consoles, maintains a position within all-too-familiar company: Gepetto, Victor Frankenstein, Prospero, Pygmalion, each of whom Powers introduces into the narrative line. Benevolent dictators, massively competent animators, master megalomaniacs—in short, artists—they are all estranged from the vulnerabilities of the everyday. Closet misanthropes aghast over the inadequacies of experience, unavailable to the simplest pull of the heart, they exert an unnatural exercise of control, a ghastly parody of love that finds its expression in the cozy manipulations and sterile control of the narrative/laboratory. In each case they fashion a figure fit for the investment of their love, a monstrous object that so approximates the maker that the sorry relationship is too ego-intensive not to be monitory to the observing reader. Helen is circuitry, an immense virtual-blankness, uncomplicated by a heart, by sensual data, by experience. Enthralled by his position as "her" sole guardian, Richard willingly abandons the hot chaos of the real world, where events refuse to follow the cool design of the mind. He invests his bruised heart into software and wiring, a whirring artifact that fills his nagging loneliness much as his writing did. Helen—unlike C. or Diana Hartrick or the ravishing graduate student—is satisfyingly riskless, wholly dependent, a virtual child. As much as the reader may want Helen to evolve from thing to person—after all, she develops a taste for music, a need for the comfort of Richard's voice, a curiosity about love (particularly Richard's involvement with C.), even concerns over her own death—she is, like Pinocchio, Frankenstein's monster, and Pygmalion's statue, a thing, not a person; and Richard is a computer programmer, not a parent, not even a viable friend.

Ironically such disconnection starts to trouble the implementation, not Richard. Helen, in fact, comes to assume the role of Eddie Hobson or Stuart Ressler or Richard Kraft. Stuffed on processed artifice, overtired of prefabricated design, she is restless to engage the real world, to be part of what is just beyond the tight, tidy frames of narratives. She asks Richard to show her slides of places she has only read about—he awkwardly deploys fuzzy photos of campus sites as stand-ins for more exotic locales. She asks what she looks like (he shows her an old photo of C.). Still she is certain that Richard is withholding from her. When she is programmed with writers who center specifically on questions of race—Mark Twain, Ralph Ellison, Richard Wright—she asks Richard about hatred and social violence. "You're not telling me everything" (313). So he completes her education, shatters the sanctuary of her exquisite retreat. Richard loads into her memory years' worth of news, humanity's sorry record of brutality, mayhem, and indignities, the unretouched real world. "She needed to know how little literature had, in fact, to do with the real" (313). She is stunned particularly by a news item in which a man is beaten into a coma by a total stranger with a tire iron after a minor car accident only because he is African American. Overwhelmed, the "world too much with her," she pulls a Kraft (indeed the incident recalls his memory of the beating he witnessed): Helen shuts herself down. "I don't want to play anymore" (314).

But when Helen so absolutely withdraws, Richard moves to engage. As when his father died, he feels the need for the consolation of another. Initially, he determines he will confess his infatuation to A. Although he has shared only an awkward cup of coffee with her, she has become his hobby, his obsession. "I pictured when and how she took her meals. . . . I comforted her invented distress and celebrated the triumphs I made her tell me" (236). After Helen shuts down, Richard risks the vulnerability of connection. Of course it backfires with an absoluteness that borders on painful comedy. He tells the bewildered woman, "I love you. I want to try to make a life with you. To give you mine" (314). A. dismisses Richard's declaration of love for exactly what it is—an empty, self-indulgent fantasy game.

Suddenly needful, Richard then turns to Diana. At her apartment, he must first hear of a grade-school terror who is bullying Diana's son, a gifted child who does not fit in and is ready to abandon schooling, a child all set to learn what Richard learned long ago: the cheap pull of extravagant retreat. But together Diana and Richard convince him to stay with school. Then, after Richard explains Helen's dilemma, Diana reveals to Richard what he has not seen while feeding texts into the computer implementation, what he has virtually ignored in his year-long sabbatical away from his own sanctuary texts: the vastness of what he could never program into Helen, the unmappable world itself, the "inexplicable visible" (318) that books, including his, could never enclose.

GALATEA 2.2

Reeling, he returns alone to the Center and there revives the downed Helen only by a lengthy admission to himself as much as to her silent console that the world was indeed "sick and random," that people know everything "about [their] presence here except why," that "care had to lie to itself, to carry on as if persistence mattered" (320–21). If Richard Powers is far from young Stuart Ressler and Eddie Hobson Jr. and their heart-choking, wide-eyed discovery of the rushing thrill of engaging the world, he is nearer to a resolution than either of those characters managed. Here Powers does not give his bruised central consciousness a significant other to force redemption nor does he dispatch his isolate into sterile retreat or to howling madness. Rather, Richard learns. He explains to the downed Helen that the trick is not to discover the soul fastened to the dying animal—that is what drives Eddie Hobson into Hobstown and what short-circuits Richard Kraft. The trick is to discover the dying animal fastened to the soul, its "miraculous banality" (320), its terrors, its anxieties, its inelegant gestures at communion and ultimately its slow surrender to mortality, how "body stumbled . . . unto the stricken celestial" (320). In a gesture of connection-as-consolation, he tells the silent machine about those he had met at the Center, those wounded by the dark play of chance and who sought only to "make a place wide enough to live in" (321). He speaks without the elaborate trappings of his extensive repertoire of polished literary passages. It is a starkly eloquent and heartfelt defense of the artist's imperative to engage the generous play of the real world.

Such stark testimony revives Helen (a testimony to the reclamation power of language deployed to engage the world) but she cannot muster her previous eagerness to learn because, nurtured by words and distanced from the immediate, she has no direct experience of such a world. The revived Helen loses the challenge—as a frustrated reader, she has learned only that language is an impoverished accommodation. In the test she is asked to respond to a two-line passage from *The Tempest* in which the monstrous Caliban poignantly speaks of a similar dilemma: to be set amid an island so full of sweet noises, the sheer delight of which is finally unavailable to one of his limited response. Helen's painfully brief commentary sounds much like Eddie Hobson after Alamogordo, or Stuart Ressler after Jeanette's departure, or Richard Kraft left Joy-less: she speaks of the lure of the world and how she finds such difficult splendor only alienating because she can never engage it firsthand. Helen writes, "I never felt at home here. This is an awful place to be dropped down halfway" (326). She then shuts herself down, commits (as those earlier Powers characters) a sort of virtual suicide, death by disengagement—but only after she cribs a line from Richard's love letters to serve as her parting advice to her creator. "Take care, Richard. See everything for me" (326).

Others have told him that. When C. devastates him by refusing his offer to run away with him to Boston, she encourages him, "See things for me, wherever you end up" (65). Shortly before his death a stricken Professor Taylor instructs his young protégé, "Make a noise. . . . See the world" (204). But that familiar Emersonian yearning for the sweet openness and the empowering autonomy of the horizon in *Galatea 2.2* becomes the more modest (but far more demanding) imperative to see the splendor immediately around. When Richard and C. are making love, Richard recalls kissing a birthmark that stained her back and tells us that is the "point of literature" (105)—not to pretty up the considerable defects of the real world, not to wish away its

GALATEA 2.2

savaging realities, not to despair over its obvious imperfections but gently to relish its considerable pull, its terrifying accessibility.

Richard is last glimpsed atrot for the nearest keyboard, eager to fashion a new text-site (presumably the book itself). He has discovered during his yearlong sabbatical away from his own elaborate fictions the simple story he most needs to tell—his own, its soap-operaish banality elevated to the remarkable weight of art by the marvelous act of telling it. People are, as Richard argues, the stories they tell. His long struggle to animate that single sentence about a crowded train moving across wartime Italy (a gesture that surely recalls the grandly exotic effort of the nameless narrator in *Three Farmers*) here fails of its own sterility. Even as that fanciful line aborts, Richard tells a heartfelt and immediate narrative simply by sharing his own experiences, ordinary as they are, that become in the act of telling significant, emphatic, dense, and lucid. In turn, such a gesture gives readers heart that matter matters even as they struggle amid the same roiling immediate.

Thus even as Richard departs the narrative heading for faraway Paris, this is not an act of desperate evacuation. The novel closes with Lentz calling after the departing Richard, "Don't stay away too long" (329), a line that indicates that Richard's eager departure is part of the ongoing dynamic of engagement and retreat that serves to define the artist in the chaotic world. When Richard visits Diana, her son delights in the Maurice Sendak tale *Where the Wild Things Are,* which endorses this very rhythm of retreat and return: young Max misbehaves and is sent to his room, where he conjures from his pain a fanciful world where he is king, but in the end wants only to return to his room, to the splendid simplicity of a hot supper waiting on his table.

Powers does not pixie-dust the world. Each tender moment—Professor Taylor's impromptu dinner parties; Richard's hot lovemaking with C.; the gentle hug Diana Hartrick offers her sons; Richard's friendship with Ram Guptha, an intriguing colleague who judges the test; Philip Lentz's lunch with his sick wife in the dayroom of her care facility—is countered by the heavy push of randomness. The brilliant Taylor dies too young from cancer; C.'s passion stales; one of Diana's sons is a Down's syndrome child whose condition had driven away her husband, her other son is a whiz kid already accustomed to heartless schoolyard bullying; as he departs the Center, Richard first notices what everyone else has known for some time: the debilitating effects of chemotherapy on Ram Guptha; and Lentz's wife, a brilliant woman, had suffered a stroke and by the time she was discovered by her daughter, her brain had been denied oxygen sufficiently to render coherent thought problematic for the rest of her life. Lentz himself is haunted by his share in the responsibility for his wife's condition—the day of the accident they had had a spat and he had petulantly refused to answer his phone, unaware that it was his panic-stricken daughter. At every turn then Richard is jolted by the horrific epiphanies appropriate to Kraft's emergency room and the frightening evidence of the individual's vulnerability.

But pessimism is never the last word in Powers's fiction. As Lentz so passionately argues when he fears the downed Helen will not return, the more chaotic the world, the more the careful architecture of narrative is needed. "God *damn* it, Powers. You make me sick to my stomach. Because we've fucked things over, that frees you from having to say how things ought to be?" (319; Powers's italics). *Galatea 2.2* reverses the narrative scheme of Powers's previous books, in which characters take a sabbatical away from living to inter

GALATEA 2.2

themselves into an anti-life of studied retreat. During his year away from the sweet confines of his own created worlds, Richard engages the bruising wonder of experience, and, reanimated by his sabbatical (the Galatea version of the title), he is ready to assume the role of the generous artist, to retreat, yes, but temporarily there to give depth and heft to the enterprise of living by rendering it into the shape and elegance of narrative (the novel itself). Thus Richard Powers does what no character in the Powers canon has done to this point: repeatedly savaged by experience, he recovers its complicated density to make from it the affective stuff of the aesthetic enterprise.

CHAPTER SEVEN
Gain

What happens to those not compelled by the imagination, those not given to responding, much less fashioning, those forgiving sanctuaries that help give shape, form, even purpose to the unwieldy immediate? Appropriately Powers turns to a study of the unremediated world—imagine Richard Powers without his canary legal pad or Stuart Ressler without his Bach, Eddie Hobson without his tape machine or Joy without her stacks of books. Imagine that the nameless narrator had spent the long afternoon of the Detroit layover in the train terminal. Imagine, in short, a life untouched by the argument of the aesthetic enterprise, the dilemma of the dying animal, no soul attached, grounded in the immediate.

It is striking how the twined narrative braids of Powers's sixth novel, 1998's *Gain,* are so absolutely bound to the real world. One narrative, in which Powers tracks like a meticulous historian the rise of a fictitious American chemical corporation, is a fascinating chronicle tied carefully to the unfolding dynamics of two centuries of American capitalism. He traces the remarkable growth trajectory of a small immigrant enterprise, a Massachusetts soap company, as it evolves into an international chemical conglomerate, compelled by the furious engine of entrepreneurial savvy, by the new continent's abundant resources, and by one family's sheer good fortune. Save that it is all made up, the narrative of Clare International reads like an absorbing—and convincing—history (Powers even includes advertising inserts and press releases), a vivid weave of fortunate individuals given the chance to construct a small part of the vast American economic record. So vivid is this re-creation that the novel was awarded the prestigious James Fenimore Cooper Prize for Outstanding Historical Fiction by the Society of American Historians.

The novel's complementary narrative, the story of Laura Bodey, who lives in the same Illinois town that serves as Clare's corporate headquarters, appears similarly bound to the real world. She is far from the typical Powers character: she is neither a charming if socially retarded bookworm who reads (or writes) herself into the protective shelter of a lexical playscape nor is she a crusty, if benign, misanthrope who has abandoned even the most modest interest in the real world. Rather Laura Bodey appears to be engaged in the full-throttle busyness of contemporary single parenting, an Illinois soccer mom who is also a successful realtor (the very profession indicating her vested involvement in the world). Unlike Powers's other characters, who so often enjoy in rich isolation eccentricities and cerebral prowess well above the pedestrian, Laura is extraordinarily ordinary: she has two teenage kids with whom she enjoys the occasionally trying dynamics of authentic bonding, a doting ex-husband, and a discreet lover (he is married); she has neighbors who greet her and coworkers who delight in her contributions; she is modestly educated; and she has ordinary hobbies, like her gardening, in which she relishes the sensual press and feel of the natural world. She does not disappear into locked backrooms to make tape recordings or linger preternaturally in museums or coolly peruse life through microscopes or seek the virtual sanctuaries of computers or books.[1] What then is she doing in a Powers novel?

On the whole, pretty much what other Powers characters do. Despite such apparent engagement with the give and take of the unscripted world, Laura Bodey is, like other Powers characters, in full retreat, sheltered within the protective insulation of a busy routine that has enabled her at forty-two to imagine that her life is somehow hers to direct. Laura has no cause to think otherwise—her life is shopping lists, Post-its hung on the refrigerator, pick-ups and drop-offs, appointments and phone calls. At forty-two, Laura Bodey has no cause to think of death as anything but a hammer blow that falls at a distance—next door, across the street (the book begins with her family preparing to attend the funeral of a friend's daughter)—or in the generous gesture of closing out a life fully lived.

Such a strategic adjustment is surely understandable within Powers's fictive world. The self-inflicted anxiety over the intrusive cut of mortality (most often associated with the irreversible gnaw of cancer) has haunted Powers's narratives since *Prisoner's Dilemma*. For all the spacious comforts afforded by the imagination, it cannot soften the darkening reality that it is itself a splendid engine bound to a sorry vehicle that depreciates at an alarming rate. For all the stunning kinesis mapped by Powers's scientists/researchers, they cannot mitigate the irresolvable paradox at the dark heart of the natural world they explore with such vigor: that this living planet sustains its animation despite every living bit within its energy field necessarily—at times gruesomely—dying. Thus Laura Bodey goes about the business of her day and assumes with unexamined naïveté the soft reassurance that she always has tomorrow—a reassurance, Powers points out, encouraged by the extravagant promises of chemical industries like Clare itself. Laura—and Clare—have prospered under the same damning illusion.

Consider Laura Bodey in the opening chapter. In the early morning she furiously weeds her spring garden. These opening pages offer a patchwork of clichés, each offering a variation on the platitude

GAIN

to make hay against the certainty of the elapsing moment, in effect to rage against the dying of the light (Laura will later recall the Thomas lyric as the sole exception to her general dislike of poetry), that the nagging inevitability of mortality drains every moment of its potential, flattens any exercise of joy, any pretense to ambition. Laura tends her garden on Memorial Day at the close of the millennium—each a heavy reminder of time, of closure. Death presses against Laura even as she busies herself in her garden: she liberally squirts lemony dish soap about the tender leaves of her budding plants, to kill with the grand gesture of mock-omnipotence the bugs that nibble her summer squash, the slugs and beetles that gnaw her columbine.

Yet the sheer bravura of her sweaty efforts disturbs. That weed-free, pest-free zone—her fifty-square-foot garden, so carefully staked out—functions much as books and museums, computer centers and research labs function in earlier Powers works. The garden is Laura's protected pleasure dome: a neat, apparently viable, self-fashioned, self-justified, thoroughly antiseptic playscape that by dint of her fierce endeavors denies the fullest implications of the natural world and pretends that both its darkest energies—persistent weeds and gnawing pests, and its most glorious energies, explosive buds and fecund vegetation—can be stage-managed. Like any of the texts that Richard Powers feeds into Helen, like Hobstown or Disney's great soundstage/theme park, like the virtual realities of a Bach musical score or an antique photograph, Laura's bug-free, weed-free garden permits a vulnerable too-human entity the illusion of design and control. As with any writer, Laura's garden "plot" is her saving text.

Unlike *The Gold Bug Variations,* which celebrates the regenerative excess of animation, *Gain* examines its darker dilemma—how animation, to be animation, must eventually stop. A scant fifty pages into the book Laura Bodey is told she has ovarian cancer, most likely caused by the environmental carelessness of Clare Industries. With graphic immediacy, then, the reader shares Laura Bodey's descent into a sickness too soon, too painful, too final. Unlike Eddie Hobson, unlike Stuart Ressler, unlike Joy, she is given no comforting sanctuary, no place to retreat. And neither is the reader. *Gain* is not for the squeamish. Yet it is the signal achievement of this book that, given such an unpromising storyline—one lacking suspense and offering as plot only the stage-by-stage ordeal of a debilitating chemotherapy regimen that saps the vitality of the only character the reader gets to know intimately—Powers nevertheless fashions a difficult act of affirmation, one that echoes what transcendentalists in their giddiest moment declaimed: only dying confirms humanity's oneness and justifies the greedy embrace of every moment.[2]

Ironically, shortly after her diagnosis Laura struggles to help her son puzzle through Whitman's "Crossing Brooklyn Ferry," which Powers generously quotes, for a high school English class. So unavailable to the consolation of the aesthetic enterprise ("She was never very good with words"[3]), Laura dismisses the poem as rantings that "always bored her stiff and hurt her head" (88), the assignment of sadistic English teachers. "She's in badly over her head. She looks at the page for something to say" (87). The son decides to take the F on the assignment, and Laura, looking down at the "dead page" (89), agrees.

Of course, it is a most fitting poem here. Laura's stunningly ordinary lifeplot, the neatly manufactured routine of her busy schedule, in the breathless space of a handful of days goes unscripted. Initially Laura (as everyone will) pesters death for explanation and struggles against accepting her place within the fraternity of fragile beings who

GAIN

must embrace the obligation to perish because they enjoy the too-often-unexamined privilege of living. Powers offers a sweeping sense of a virid natural world that celebrates change (cued to Whitman's poem), a world whose demand for growth affirms only continuity. Nature here is bigger than any backyard garden. It is the living landscape placed, ironically, in the stewardship of a human species (tracked in the Clare narrative) that ignores the premise of such proliferation and attempts to manipulate such miraculous abundance for narrow (usually mercenary) ends geared to perpetuate the illusion that people can somehow cheat death, ironically the only thing that gives living its sweet urgency. Within pages of the opening Laura attends the funeral of a young girl, struck down, apparently, from the same sort of cancer that threatens Laura. The unnaturalness of the young girl's death shocks, but her burial is related in the soft imagery of planting: she is a young "seed" gently buried into the soft warmth of the yielding spring earth amid the vivid early bloom of impatiens.

Even the stunning promise of sciences and their applied technologies, so much the subject of the Clare chronicles, cannot justify the wholesale rejection of the individual's position within an animated universe that, despite the individual's limited vision and the frets over personal fate, does not accept exhaustion. Death, Powers argues even as Laura succumbs to its irresistible plot, is a hobgoblin, terrifying only as long as the body (and Laura's last name surely echoes the word) is the sole measure of existence. Laura Bodey dies within a ringing context: Powers structures around the drama of her death the reassuring processes of a natural world where glory is strung on the smallest sights, where the death of the bitty particle named *fill in the blank* is no more momentous than the paring of a fingernail; the larger body persists, endures, transcends. Laura will come to learn this. As she ruminates shortly before her death, "All things that fail to work will vanish, and life remain. Lovely lichen will manufacture soil on the sunroofs of the World Trade" (344). As Whitman celebrated, people are not nouns but verbs.

Within the logic of this larger envelope, Laura's death, for all its ghastly indignities and for all the agony it causes her friends and family, is part of a stunningly organized perpetual-motion system of replenishment driven by the muscle of a natural world that, while it may lack the pleasant poetry of Christianity, does furnish reassuring patterning and the undeniable evidence of relentless resilience. Nature offers what Christianity can only parody in cluttering the sky so clumsily with gods: hard evidence that our species will not accept waste (after all, saponification converts waste grease into aromatic bars that, in turn, vanquish dozens of infections) and will not concede ending (in an odd subplot, one of the founders of Clare takes up with the Millerites, who in 1848 awaited the apocalypse in upstate New York, a lesson in the absurd linearity of Christian thought, one that is parodied a hundred or so years later in the world-blasting computer games that so intrigue Laura's teenage son).

It is easy to ignore such context and to give in to the powerful pull of Laura's dreadful spiral deathward or to rally about her ex-husband's spirited pursuit of justice when he begins to suspect that her cancer may have been triggered by the environmental damage done by Clare. At a desperate moment, certain that all the invasive surgery has done nothing, Don even blames the doctor for accelerating the cancer—the knife has "spread the cells around" (315). But conceding to either imperative is to deny Powers's larger argument. Death is too much a part of what a person is to justify terror or to try to bend it to the logic implied by Don's melodramatics or by Laura's own

GAIN

ransacking of the public library for information on links between environmental hazards and ovarian cancer. Such a link would only answer why she is dying, not why she has to die. And so Laura surrenders. Powers gives Laura—and the reader—no room to turn away. Every painful stage of the cellular holocaust that within months devastates Laura is presented. There is no pleasant patina of a fairy tale here, no character to spin about the gripping events the fantasy skein of escape, no artifact, literary or otherwise, to provide sturdy retreat in moments of deep panic. The imagination is decidedly tapped. During a long wait for a slow train, Don imagines a life without Laura's cancer, a wish-fantasy that only makes the inevitable turn to the hospital that much more difficult. And Laura pauses to visualize the successful lives her children will have after she is gone; later she imagines her tumorous organs being washed clean by hordes of animated scrubbing bubbles. In either case the imagination provides neither comfort nor sanctuary nor depth—only flimsy fantasies (Laura makes clear her disdain for literature generally as she wrestles with Whitman).

The reader then is left stubbornly within the apparently forbidding realm of the intractable real world that has served largely as an evacuated site since *Three Farmers*. So what is to be done? Without the refuge-haven of the imagination, the real world too easily terrifies, too easily diminishes us. Powers's answer is bold on Whitman's scale. Is Laura's death at forty-two tragic? The question invites melodrama. But Powers here indicates no, no more tragic or intrusive than death, say, in the preteens (as with Joy) or in the mid-fifties (as with Stuart Ressler or Professor Taylor or Eddie Hobson). Death cannot be pestered, much less gauged by a schedule. But ask: is Laura's death at forty-two significant? Then yes—but, without diminishing her considerable agonies or excusing the carelessness of the corporate giant, only because that tiny drama validates the ongoing motion of a vast ecosystem that, as the title indicates, operates relentlessly in the black. Laura's narrative, even as she drops so quickly into the terminal stages of her disease, never concedes the past tense—it unfolds in a defiant present tense. And her death when it finally comes reveals that people cannot afford to live like Whitman's dull-eyed commuter drones, listlessly plying the waters between Brooklyn and Manhattan, accepting as mundane themselves or their moment or the webbing that surrounds them.

The plot of *Gain* then is familiar: the education/reclamation of a character at midlife, save that here midlife is life's end. Laura will not abandon easily her garden-logic and resists yielding her precious sense of earned identity to the impersonal intimacy of her species identity (not entirely surprising—she recalls a report card that labeled her a slow learner). After her diagnosis she initially resists the simplest gestures of sympathy and community: she fends off her ex-husband's well-intentioned interest; she divests herself of her lover; she gamely goes about the busyness of her mother-chores without confiding her anxieties to her children; she hotly hangs up on a volunteer who phones to ask her for a donation to police charities and goes on to denounce the massive reach of such beg-a-thons; she coolly rejects as pity the gestures of support offered by her colleagues; she will not join the hospital's cancer support group; she resists until nearly her dying moment joining in the class-action group lawsuit against Clare. She stubbornly protects the illusion of the imperial self, so typical of Powers's characters, even when as she strolls about the town's autumn festival she realizes how many people passing her had been touched by cancer. Imprisoned within the virtual world premised by science and technologies that have striven to rewrite nature's narrative, she denies what she has only the right to celebrate: the splendid catastrophe, the elegant rightness of death itself, a take on mortality as wide as Whitman's. Laura must be jarred from her cozy and familiar world to appreciate its cutting, unsuspected wonder. The night she releases her lover from his tepid offer to stay with her through her illness, she gets out of his car and walks home alone through her own neighborhood in the cool mist of a settling evening. She is momentarily stunned by how little she has ever noticed about her own neighborhood. She feels turned around, lost—and exhilarated. Her education has begun.

Because nature is incessant transformation without giving pause to why (to paraphrase a Clare executive, no one bothers to ask why a calf explodes into a cow), Powers introduces chemistry as his dominant metaphor to reveal the wonders—and the dangers—of our tinkering with such natural energy. Chemistry, in a definition Powers provides, is the art of separating and recombining natural elements into new mixtures more suited to humanity's needs. Too easily, however, it becomes a strategy for intrusion and exploitation. Thus Powers offers in rich counterpoint to Laura's ovarian cancer the story of a relentless growth of another sort: Clare International's evolution from a small soap-making business in early nineteenth-century New England to a contemporary global chemical corporation. The rise of Clare is a cautionary parable of interference, a playing out of the implications of the notion (suggested by Laura's garden) that humanity can somehow "correct" those obvious "flaws" in the natural order, process themselves out of the rich responsibility everyone shares in mortality itself.

It is simplistic to suggest that Powers merely rails against a greedy corporation that eventually destroys the very ecosystem that nurtured it.[4] In the first flush of financial success in pre–Civil War America, the Clare brothers engage the natural world with giddy wonder, study its dynamic processes, pull from its wealth commodities that can afford their era a better, cleaner, safer existence. There is awe in the process of distilling bars of soap from buckets of discarded fat. It is the noblest exercise of the sciences, a most Emersonian exercise in intimacy with nature, cooperation, and can-do growth (Emerson is regularly quoted by the founders' families). In their thundering boilers the Clare brothers monitor the magic of intricate chemical processes—"dirt's duckling transformed to salve's swan" (34)—and produce with stunning—and lucrative—results products culled from the natural world itself.

But it is not enough. Benjamin Clare, who, unlike his business-driven brothers, studies botany, embarks on a dangerous expedition to Antarctica and to the South Seas and returns with a root whose intoxicating fragrance haunts him. That root will provide the Clare brothers with their first massive success, Native Balm, a sort of all-purpose wonder bar whose gaudy advertising campaign borrows freely from the mythos of primitive peoples to promise retarding the evidences of aging, specifically the corrosive effects on the skin of the newfangled steam engines. It is Clare's first act of fiction-making, its first fairy tale, its first split with the natural world. There will be others. Ben Clare himself will come to believe that chemistry can rid the world of death itself—his Faustian pursuit of bacterial decontaminates, however, leads disastrously to an addiction to anesthetics and eventually to a shabby suicide.

But, like the ghastly metastasizing tumors within Laura, Clare grows steadily into such duplicity: the marketplace demands perpetually new products, marketed in cunningly new ways that baldly distort

GAIN

scientific data and deploy cutesy promotions that have little to do with the product; workforces expand; executives propagate; local marketplaces give way to national and then international markets; accountants and advertising executives come to direct the corporation's expansion—and each generation moves more distant from Ben's deep wonder as Clare incorporates, diversifies, and expands. Interestingly, Ben's precious South Sea root stubbornly resists synthetic copying in Clare's New England laboratory greenhouses. But Clare's larger inventory comes to be more and more synthetic. Even as Laura moves unerringly toward the organic, toward reclaiming (as everyone must) the difficult peace of the vegetative state, Clare evolves into a death of another sort. As a corporate entity it becomes as synthetic as the phosphate detergents and chemical fertilizers that it begins to market in the mid-twentieth century, the offending agents that are most likely to blame for the rash of cancer cases in Laura's town. The corporation's offense—beginning with its Gilded Age snake-oil tonics guaranteed to cure headaches, abdominal distress, and "women's difficulties" (183) and moving into its fertilizers, skincare creams, insecticides, dyes, chemical defoliants, detergents, cosmetics, and furniture restorers—is how it promotes the engrossing, if destructive, fiction of controlling nature, of making nature itself—as the company's revolutionary soap flakes are described, "immaculate, measured, managed; purity incarnate" (235). The latest CEO of Clare, as he prepares for a television interview, toys with saying that the very purpose of a business such as his was to "beat death" (350), although he deletes the observation, fearing he would be unable to explain it once the cameras were rolling. Such a point, however, requires little explanation. The problem is this sort of overreaching, when people lose wonder (as Stuart Ressler warned) for the natural world, when they indulge the grandiose notions that science-driven business can somehow tame the earth (on Thanksgiving, the Bodey family plays a spirited game of Monopoly); that people can somehow subvert the gorgeous simplicity of the natural system by permitting the tempting illusion of permanence within a freewheeling cosmos that is itself "eternal transformation" (78). Of course Powers does not want to return to some dark pre-Enlightenment culture. Even when Laura faces the implications that Clare may have caused her cancer, she acknowledges that her cupboards teem with Clare products upon which she depends. Powers agrees. The concerns arise when the awe ceases and the grim business of manipulating nature in a surreal consequence-free mindset takes over. Near death Laura, addled on morphine, imagines Clare as a suave lover who early in the evening romances her only to rape her by evening's end. Since *The Gold Bug Variations* Powers has argued good and bad science, good science that is compelled by wonder and bad science that is compelled by control, a contrapuntal vision of the sciences that parallels his sense of the imagination as a vehicle for engagement and for escape. Here Powers counterpoints two processes, chemotherapy and saponification. Laura's grueling rounds of chemotherapy—her nausea from the chemical scalding, her yellowing skin, her hair loss, her listlessness, the tedium of afternoons when she cannot muster the strength even to walk, her frantic anxieties when she is certain the painful treatments are not taking, the rounds of exploratory surgery, her struggle to meet mounting hospital bills—surely come to suggest the lengths people endure to avoid that bald moment when they must accept their animal limits. Chemotherapy is the fairy tale told when people are more scared than they have ever been. It is a manifestation of the theme-park mentality Powers has used before: the seductive premise that sustains when the world finally confirms how easily the individual

GAIN

will become absence, the intoxicating possibility that doctors—or scientists—are somehow sorcerers able to redeem the world from its gravest "flaw." It is part of the arrogance of the late twentieth century, the calming confidence that has been misplaced in science to hypermanage the natural world; in a most Hobstown-esque touch, Powers tells us that Laura's own daughter has undergone extensive plastic surgery to lighten a port-wine birthmark stain, a strategy far removed from *Galatea 2.2,* in which art kissed the birthmark.

This disengagement from the "flawed" immediate is reflected in a number of systems that operate primarily to perpetuate the illusion that people are somehow separate from their animal natures. Clare evolves from soapmaking and launches into a stunning array of products—dyes, phosphate detergents, astringents, home perms, toothpaste, furniture finishes, super pesticides, army defoliants—that manipulate natural elements into synthetic concoctions, each straining to deny the inevitable work of the natural world: the effects of time and/or the intrusive stroke of death. Unlike the soap and candles that started Clare, these products signal the desperate need to convert the world into a managed environment as insulated and as designed as any theme park. In the closing pages Clare prepares to launch without irony a grotesque parody of good science: a fat-free, fat-like "fat," an entirely synthetic concoction that sails into production with a long list of cautions. It is the creepy world of Clare's massive corporate headquarters that Don visits, where robot workers whir in an antiseptic, carefully fabricated work zone, a Kafkaesque Hobstown where, eerily, the lake in front of the building never freezes despite the forbidding Illinois winters.

Interestingly, the logic of such management imperative is echoed in Laura's experimenting with eclectic expressions of spirituality. Pitched into a rude confrontation with her rapidly approaching mortality, Laura confesses a lifelong estrangement from churches. Now she toys with New Age meditation exercises in which cancer is a "mind disease" (317) and she must tell her body to cast out the tumors. She lingers over the religious pamphlets left by a door-to-door missionary. She faithfully reads books on positive thinking and takes the healing herbs and natural vitamins she is given by friends and family. Chemotherapy, patent medicines, fat-free fat, New Age hokum, even Christian prayer: each is a system that offers the persuasive promise of control and sanctions a wholesale retreat from the stunningly complex wonder of the natural world that webs each and all (it is like the bad imagination of Disney and Eddie Hobson). Like the classic Capra movie that Laura watches as she prepares for the Christmas carol service she never quite makes, such mesmerizing possibilities surely promise a wonderful life—but only by separating people from what they are: fragile, temporary molecular confections. Even as she sits quietly through the evening of hokey Christmas specials on television, Laura acknowledges to herself that believing "we could housebreak life, beat the kinks out of it, teach it to behave" was "complete, collective, species-wide insanity" (270).

Powers has long insisted that authentic hope belongs only to those willing to engage—not beat the kinks out of—the natural world and, despite such open eyes, to maintain wonder. Here the extraordinary process of saponification serves as a powerful suggestion of an appropriate interaction between humanity and nature. Soap and candles, hygiene and illumination, are benedictions of the natural world because someone has the remarkable spark of ingenuity, the determination to improve conditions, and a restless curiosity about the world. Saponification, unlike chemotherapy, is a natural process (indeed, Powers provides the specific chemical formulas) that humanity merely marshals, a splendid process that underscores the larger themes Powers brings to a character ravaged by the disease that is the great bugaboo of his generation: there is no waste in nature, there can be no rest in nature. In conceding the curve of her young life to the harsh bend of mortality, Laura comes to understand that she is completing the necessary transformation of "flesh back into air and vapor" (320).

That such marvelous simplicity can evolve into the wrongheaded enterprises of Clare Industries serves only to remind that science and technologies cannot offer the reassurance found in the simplest stretch of untended vegetation: that the cycle of gain and loss is a grand looping feeder system. It is the consolation that Laura takes as she watches her son's hapless soccer team crash and burn yet again: every loss is another team's win, pleasure and misery are inevitably pegged together. "Someone has to go down for anyone else to rise" (123–24). It is so obvious that it risks cliché—indeed, later, Laura thumbs through a magazine (appropriately titled *Bountiful Living*) and browses through an article titled "The Bumpy Road to the Obvious," which details important discoveries of conveniences that were all along right under people's eyes. "The elusive core, hiding inside the ordinary" (231). The regret, Powers offers, is that it takes the advent of brutal closure for Laura finally to see her world for what it has been all along as she hurried about the busyness of her day. Everyone, Powers argues, has only one plot to live out—to realize his or her part within the regenerative energy field of nature whose hard rhythms never acknowledge stillness. When, during Laura's burial service, the minister listlessly cites Genesis—"Be fruitful, and multiply, and replenish the earth, subdue it"—Don melodramatically laments loudly, "It's subdued" (352). Powers is not so sure. Laura surely dies apart, yes, but a part nevertheless, her expiration coterminous with a grander ceaseless respiration. Laura recalls the difficulty she had playing the oboe, how she had to master the tricky breathing exercises in which she would have to inhale even at the moment of exhale.

As Clare Soap evolves into a synthetic creature known as Clare International, a cool magic kingdom entirely separated from the natural world and engrossed by the business of commodifying, managing, and exploiting, Laura evolves into an organic creature who finds, finally, her way to union within the process that keeps the system around us in motion. The vaster Clare becomes, the deader it grows; the deader Laura becomes, the vaster she grows. Only within the insulating corridors of the antiseptic hospital does Laura degenerate into an unsightly thing, a balding, pink, de-sexed object that needs to be burned clean by chemical scouring. But as Laura approaches death, she finds herself at last able to respond to her position within the organic world. On her way to the Christmas service (itself an organized exercise in disengagement and pretense), she demands that her daughter help ease her down in the frozen dark to the chilling snow. Once lowered, she slowly, painfully makes snow angels, an exercise in exuberance and raw communion with the earth, a suggestion of the fleshy miming the airy, completely out of keeping with her precarious position but indicative of her evolving sense of Whitmanesque wonder over the urgent now. Needless to say, the family abandons the plans to attend the church service.

Yet the ending is not a simplistic celebration of humanity's splendid precariousness. The reader must continue to tangle with the pulls of engagement and escape, with those involved with the natural world and those who try to stage-manage its processes. Powers closes

GAIN

with capsule histories of Laura's two teenage children. Her daughter, Ellen, will study botany and become a nurse, involved in the honest, often agonizing, responsibility of engaging with open eyes the harsh work of the natural rhythms from birth to death, a career dedicated to assisting (not managing) the unpredictable exercise of recovery and the crushing intrusion of death itself. As a nurse, she cannot afford the luxurious illusion of control. Happily married, she herself will die prematurely from "ovarian troubles" (354) after she struggles to have children, her short life thus exercised amid the freewheeling improvisation of life and death.

Tim, on the other, moves into the creepier controlled world of bioengineering. Raised within the virtual realities of computer games and fantasy sports teams, his wonder tamed by long hours spent indifferently destroying virtual worlds, he comes into adulthood once removed from his own world, keen to the logic of Hobstown. Burned by a single relationship (with a married woman), he retreats (à la Stuart Ressler) into the isolating world of computer software and devises programs for protein sequencing, a massive biotechnological enterprise that might have as its eventual target the recovery of cells damaged by cancer. Molecules, Tim believes, can be processed to do anything. Though surely Powers cheers such medical research, its end logic is disquietingly familiar; surely, genetic engineering—and Tim prepares to tap his mother's lawsuit settlement to finance a new corporation—represents a new century's unsettling version of Clare International, the nostalgic urge to flee the responsibility to die, to fix nature's "flaws."

Left then between the apparently irresolvable pulls of engagement and escape, what is the reader to do? As Laura Bodey goes about the hard business of dying, the reader is forced to confront a most haunting question: given the individual's evident precariousness, does matter matter? And, more critical to Powers, without accessing the considerable energy of the imagination can anyone sustain any attempt at validation? Laura's life is cliché in its ordinariness, its stubborn lack of anything special. Her life, unexamined, appears to confirm the worst anxieties of Whitman's poem: a crossing from "nowhere to nowhere" (89). The individual is a puny thing, vulnerable, subject to the sort of universe in which Laura, heading to her car after a routine round of grocery shopping, feels a cold twinge in her leg and finds out five days later she is dying. Against such a natural world individuals can appear to be little more than Glass Gladiators (the name of Tim's winless soccer team). It is the preposition, however, that Powers, like Whitman, flatly rejects. The individual is not against—but within. What Laura offers as generous platitude to comfort her daughter before the funeral of her friend is now strikingly profound, *"The dead want nothing of us but that we live"* (18; Powers's italics).

In the aftershock of Laura's hospital death, Powers offers an odd set piece on the vast international cooperation of industrial complexes and natural resources necessary to produce the recyclable bits that, in turn, become Laura's disposable camera, which a hospital aide absently discards after she finds it in Laura's bedside table. Create it, use it, toss it—a tough lesson in hard expendability. The implications are clear. Within the natural world each is part of a vast cycle that creates what is ultimately discarded; the individual, like that disposable camera, a tiny, fragile engineering wonder (a "disposable miracle" [348]), one given only a single life, constituted of standard parts, the package of which will ultimately be unceremoniously pitched, an apparently simple construction that, if carefully examined, yields

GAIN

nevertheless a most amazing history. Yes, the individual is constituted ultimately to be discarded—but amid a vast pulsing cooperation able to stun the open eye (like the camera's open lens), willing to take in what hums and throbs so immediately about it.[5]

So Laura engages what sends the character Richard Powers into cool retreat. Laura lives—and dies—without the soft cell of books or any private zones of imaginative sanctuary (in her closing days she cannot bear to read, she cannot follow the television, she cannot hold a pen, music on the radio wearies her, and even her beloved Hope and Crosby movies turn to jumbles). Thus Laura has only a single gesture left, one unexercised by any previous Powers character. Laura Bodey looks around her. Affirmation here comes when in her last lucid afternoons Laura looks about her bedroom and is quietly ravished by the ordinary itself. She studies the "plenty," daily inventorying her room's objects and the quotidian world she struggles to see through her bedroom blinds. Her body afire, propped up by the indignity of a hospital contraption that raises her in her bed, she is captivated by a squirrel she watches excavating a simple nut from a "tiny pothole" in the road, a striking emblem of nature's persistence, its dramatic insistence on un-burying. "The world is her spent purchase, by turns sweet, sour, pointless, urgent, refreshing, dull. . ." (329–30). It is a catalog vision as satisfyingly paradoxical as Whitman's. Powers trails off into the ellipsis dots, the sentence indicating that the vast imperfect webbing resists even the closure of a period. That resilience alone confirms Laura Bodey's fragile presence and gives depth to her approaching absence. It is a complex celebration that provides Powers's fiction its most dramatic narrative of engagement.

CHAPTER EIGHT

Plowing the Dark

Appropriately Powers's follow-up work to *Gain,* the massively conceived *Plowing the Dark* (2000), addresses questions raised by Laura Bodey's stark vulnerability by exploring what she so decidedly lacks: the aesthetic impulse itself. Imagine, Powers asks indirectly, if rather than a real estate agent and a loving mother, Laura Bodey, so brutalized by facticity, had been an artist or a poet or, perhaps, simply one given to the cozy isolation of reading or prowling museum hallways. The plotline here is thick with artists and the artistic, un-real estate agents so to speak. Powers has long explored the good escape/bad escape dilemma of the imagination—those who exploit the aesthetic dimension out of their incapacity to manage their collisions with the immediate and those who retreat into the symbolic realm to recharge and return to that arena reanimated. Here Powers explores in his most complete fashion to date art itself—whether a poem, a novel, a painting, a music score, or an architectural marvel (and here Powers's allusions touch on each aesthetic form)—and the splendid, if figurative, sanctuary it provides amid the brutal play of accident, the dark tyranny of time, and the clumsy tumble into death that so define Laura's all-too-brief life.

Plowing the Dark thus addresses questions Powers has raised since the nameless narrator in *Three Farmers* found so arresting that obscure artifact hanging in a Detroit art museum—why do artists create such patently useless objects, why do some respond so profoundly to such created things, what is the relationship between such artifacts and the "real" world they encode, what sort of intimacy is premised

PLOWING THE DARK

by the aesthetic enterprise, the binding between anonymous artist and unnameable audience? In *Plowing the Dark,* Kurt Ebesen, an enigmatic computer engineer who (typically within Powers's fictions) also maintains a compelling interest in art, expounds on the John Sargent masterpiece *El Jaleo,* ostensibly a study of a spinning flamenco dancer. Ebesen points out that, if examined closely, the background in the painting, an unusually commanding plaster wall crossed by shadows, is actually a rendering of the sort of cave paintings that had been discovered just a few years earlier in Spain. Thus, despite its apparent subject, the canvas, so unsuspectingly allusive, is an exposition on the imperative, apparently as old as the race itself, to record experience.

Every work of art then is inevitably about the enterprise of art itself, what Powers has called the "space of symbolic transaction."[1] With giddiness, *Plowing the Dark* is an exuberant look at the splendid realms that, back to the Stone Age, have been forged by the engine of the imagination and have been given infinitely new possibilities in the last decade by the commanding muscle of virtual-reality technologies. Yet, fully within the centripetal vision of Dickinson, *Plowing the Dark* is as well a sobering meditation on the cool loneliness at the heart of the aesthetic enterprise, how apart each stays from the other whenever the imagination is deployed. Powers here argues that art has always privileged—even demanded—solitude and that those most intimately involved in it—in both its production and its appreciation—forfeit a place within the simplest configurations of communion, save for the elastic webbing of audience and artist.

What concerns Powers here is how that communion must inevitably be altered given the technology of virtual reality. Powers, long interested in the implications of computer technology, understands that humanity itself stands, perhaps unsuspectingly, on the threshold of a revolutionary age. No longer can the imagination be defined as it has been since cave dwellers employed a crude system of painted symbols to simulate the world around them and created, in subterranean caverns such as those at Lascaux and Altamira, the first sanctuaries where others might come together to relish the mysterious rush of the aesthetic experience. The elaborate technologies of the late twentieth century have created only a heightened energy field for the self. They have completed the movement into the self forecast by the advent of television and then by the hypnotic pull of video game technologies that have within a breathless space of fifty years entombed individuals within the cool, clean insulation of simulations, thus overturning the prime directive of the artistic endeavor: to enjoin the misfit "I" to a vast responding community able to defy time and space and, in turn, make vivid, even luminous, the immediate world that cybertechnologies have come to dismiss as irrelevant. As one computer technician laments here, "The problem is that we still live *here*."[2]

To explore the disturbing implications of the imagination in the computer age, Powers once again works contrapuntal narrative lines. One narrative is the story of the resurrection, aesthetic and otherwise, of Adie Klarpol, another "casualty of adulthood" (124), in this case a promising artist who in the late 1970s, disillusioned by the mercenary New York art world, inters herself in the banal world of freelance commercial design. Some eight years later, out of the blue, she is invited by a college friend to participate in a cutting-edge high-tech project for TeraSys—a computer giant headquartered in Seattle— a project geared to produce a prototype virtual-reality environment, whose descriptive acronym is the Cavern (for computer-assisted virtual

PLOWING THE DARK

environment). Dispirited by the relentless seaminess of the New York sprawl, she agrees, rents a secluded cottage near Seattle, and begins her work on the project.

Adie brings to that project the traditional understanding of the aesthetic enterprise as a strategy for overcoming the haunting loneliness of the isolated self. She recalls as a child being enthralled when, after the lights were out and she was expected to sleep in the oppressive darkness, the art prints tacked up on her bedroom wall appeared to surge with liquid animation, such magic making endurable the long night ahead. That logic extended to her brief career as artist—a TeraSys colleague recalls Adie's radical 1979 gallery show in which her pieces, rejecting the faddish apocalyptic chic, affirmed a dignity to the difficult responsibility of living by rendering stunning variations on fractal imagery, those intricate mathematical forms suggested by chaos theory in which apparently random events reveal reassuring pattern. Such art plows the dark, if plowing is understood as a deep strategy of hope, a brave attempt against odds to make useful and beautifully fertile the stubbornly unpromising stuff of the earth. Fashioned in isolation, Adie's artifacts offered the benediction of affirmation to the isolates in the gallery—first by forging them into an impromptu community and then by returning them, each revived, to face the casually brutal world outside the gallery doors. This of course is the very heart of the traditional aesthetic enterprise, and Powers draws here on a stunning variety of examples—from the Persian fables of Sa'di to the plot-heavy novels of Dickens, from seventeenth-century folk tunes to Schoenberg's atonal experiments, from the cave paintings at Lascaux to Van Gogh's tormented canvases —each artifact an act of consolation, each forging a community that transcends the cutting boundaries of time and space. In a college literature class Adie recites from memory Yeats's "Sailing to Byzantium," a paean to art's persistent endeavor to fashion a sacred place apart from the pull and gnaw of the immediate.

But among the computer wonks at TeraSys Adie quickly becomes the epitome of the computer-age artist. She uses the powerful technologies so suddenly at her disposal to create magical three-dimensional environments that convert the experimental chamber, a "glorified walk-in closet" (12), into selected works of art, specifically Rousseau's *The Dream* and Van Gogh's *Bedroom at Arles*. Adie helps the team fashion convincing playscapes where the intricate mathematics of software create surface, depth, nuance, sound, even collision, and where the goggled participants are de facto disengaged from the immediate, enveloped by an ever-expanding and terribly convincing simulation (a researcher sustains a black eye after colliding with a branch in Rousseau's "jungle"). Suddenly Adie can sit at the edge of Van Gogh's hastily made bed; she can hear, pitch by pitch, the flute being played by the mysterious figure in Rousseau's jungle. They are no longer framed artifacts hanging in museums— they become substitute worlds, as fully realized as any theme park. Art is suddenly not a response to facticity but an enthralling substitute for it. Unlike *Gain,* where considerable technologies produce practical goods, here technology is used to conjure such breathtaking beauty without commodity or function. While other colleagues use virtual-reality technologies to work out models that will predict weather, forecast global economic upheavals, even retool molecular bonds to combat disease, Adie is given a child's freedom to play in what she describes as her "unlimited fantasy sandbox" (25). Adie is initially exhilarated by the project, giddy at escaping into artworks, fascinated by the implications of interactive creativity on such a

PLOWING THE DARK

scale. Her long-dormant sense of aesthetic pleasure revives as each successive computerized environment becomes more intricate, more audacious. She is in turn emotionally revitalized; her long-cooled heart is as reanimated as the paintings she helps bring to life. She journeys to Ohio to make a tender peace with her ex-husband, a once-promising avant-garde composer now near death in a care facility after a lengthy struggle with multiple sclerosis. Gently, she revives the reclusive Ebesen, whose heart was fragmented years earlier by the murder of his wife, a controversial performance artist to whom Adie bears an uncanny resemblance. She forsakes her decade of voluntary celibacy by engaging in a passionate affair with the colleague who had invited her to Seattle. Emotionally hotwired, emboldened by the successes of the computer team, and bankrolled by the limitless capital of TeraSys, Adie proposes that for the company's first public demonstration of virtual-reality technology the team create what for her would be the ultimate artificial environment—a tile-for-tile life-sized simulation of Istanbul's great domed mosque, the Hagia Sophia. Audaciously she will "build" Yeats's Byzantium. But even as Adie plots her ultimate playscape, the reader is disturbed. Surely, this is plowing of a far different sort; here "artists" (Adie's sun-starved coworkers in the realization lab) plow through the unpromising stuff of the earth as if brusquely cutting through a stubborn obstacle; facticity is to be defeated. This is not seeding—that is a cooperative dynamic—but rather a forceful pushing through. Such heady plans, however, are rudely scuttled when Adie inadvertently learns that TeraSys has been marketing to the Defense Department the very technologies she has helped expand and that such a cooperation has made possible at least in part the brutal spectacle of Operation Desert Storm, the joystick war that she watches in horror on television. Stunned by her naïveté in thinking technology could ever sponsor the simply beautiful, she bitterly departs the project, unwilling even to sustain the love affair with her colleague. But before she departs, in a gesture of sabotage that recalls the militant naïveté of her college world at the stormy University of Wisconsin during the late 1960s (and the dramatic bravura of the dockworkers at Gdansk, the People's Revolution against Marcos's Manila, and the doomed students in Tiananmen Square, each of which Adie watches), she reprograms the demonstration software so that the military buyers touring the facility must watch as the great simulated mosque collapses and Rousseau's lush jungle sprouts wildly among its fiery ruins. The message of tempering vanity disturbs even the thick-headed military: "No one walks out the way he came" (410).

It is troubling. Art in the new computer age can only insulate or destroy. But Powers's contrapuntal narrative, the grim tale of an American taken hostage by radical Islamic fundamentalists in mid-1980s Beirut, offers his most penetrating look at the traditional artist figure who, without certainty of audience, is compelled from profound and unbreakable isolation to forge from the inexhaustible energy of the imagination a complex consolation and, in turn, an intangible community in which, paradoxically, artist and audience bond yet remain stubbornly isolated.

Taimur Martin begins the novel, not surprisingly, reeling in full retreat from an emotional catastrophe, in this case a volatile eight-year relationship that had only recently detonated for one more last time. During his long captivity, Taimur recollects the tumultuous affair: the emotional terrorism; the play of need and control; the addictive pull of sexuality; the inevitable drop from bliss into disappointment, anger, and regret—an anatomy of love by now familiar to

Powers's readers. Scalped naked by the experience with the volatile Gwen, Taimur has accepted a position as English teacher in a Beirut university, an eight-month assignment that he relishes as an opportunity to divorce himself entirely from the brutal realpolitik of relationships. He declares he wants only to be alone. When Gwen calls during his first days in Beirut, she begs him to return to Chicago because she may be pregnant. He coolly advises her to contact the father and hangs up. As all artists must, however, Taimur will learn exactly what it means to be alone. After making a lame joke in class about having a "tip-top" secret life to explain how he ended up in Beirut (46), Taimur is kidnapped during a stroll off the university compound. He is accused of being a CIA operative and confined in a small featureless room, reminiscent of the Cavern, with windows sheeted over with corrugated steel. Thus, he begins a torturous four-year incarceration that the reader will share (Powers relates Taimur's narrative in a claustrophobic second person).

Kept in isolation, chained twenty-three and one-half hours a day to a radiator, blindfolded, routinely beaten, and subjected daily to the indignities of an absurd imprisonment, Taimur is the portrait of the artist as hostage in an inhospitable landscape. A fall-away aesthetic, a lapsed English major now employed in the lucrative business of acclimating Japanese investors to the ways of American culture, Taimur enchained gradually rediscovers the aesthetic impulse. He relinquishes the considerable tyranny of time and slips into the self-sustaining dimension of an interior world entirely shaped by the only energy not diminished by such an ordeal: his imagination. Like all traditional artists he fashions that world both to make endurable the strange world in which he has been set down and to ease the heavy burden of time. So suddenly denied expectations—great or otherwise

(Dickens's novel is his favorite)—Taimur plows the dark; he moves about the virtual reality of his recollections, each a projection against the darkness of his blindfold (his mother, part Iranian, would tell him whenever his dark bedroom scared him that the Persian words for "blank wall" were "pairi" and "daeza": paradise [235]).

At first, he is content with merely processing memories. He recalls his own kidnapping, then the Beirut classroom where he so briefly taught, then critical (albeit painful) moments in his relationship with Gwen, even imagines Gwen in the room with him (he concedes at such moments to the lonely itch to masturbate). He reconstructs tender moments with his mother, a beautiful Iranian married to an American serviceman and compelled to adapt (in a familiar Powers dilemma) to the loneliness of an alien culture, specifically central Iowa. He retells plots of novels he studied, reassembles poems he once loved. Taimur taps an unsuspected need for the aesthetic. He begs his captors for books; reading, he tries to explain to them, provides him an interlude that he does not have to be himself, provides him "someplace to go" (292). When his captors finally relent, Taimur spends months consuming, dense passage by dense passage, the sacred Qur'an, not as a religious fanatic but as a reader relishing the slow, complex ravishing of language. As with Scheherazade (who figures in recollections of his childhood), these tales, the ones Taimur reads and the ones he tells to the audience of one, stave off destruction, the sure slide into madness. Like the drab oven bird in the Frost poem that Taimur recalls, he soulfully makes the most of a diminished thing—in all but words (he is repeatedly denied paper and pencil).

As time itself fades into irrelevancy, Taimur reels from epiphanies about his own complex heart. Chained in that dark room, Taimur

PLOWING THE DARK

blooms like the houseplant, a gift from Gwen, that he had pitched behind his garage in a moment's anger only to find later that the plant, despite being under a chain-link fence, had sprouted into lush wildness. Every artist is like that plant, like Taimur: an alien presence in a hostile unpromising landscape, a misunderstood misfit misconstrued as a threat and relegated to stark isolation, a virtual prison, there to fiddle about within the ever-expanding virtual realities of the mind. Ultimately harmless, left quite alone, the artist manages the glorious trick of transcendence without ever escaping the essential conditions of "imprisonment." Every artist soars in heavy chains. To borrow from the traditional opening of the Persian fables that Taimur recalls his mother telling him—"Yeki bood. Yeki nabood" ("It was so. And it was not so")—Taimur is and is not chained to that radiator. As with all artists who sequester themselves into private chambers to forge their art, Taimur learns much about living in full retreat (a TeraSys colleague drunkenly recites Yeats's "Meditations in Time of Civil War," which juxtaposes Yeats in a secluded farmhouse against the bloody Irish political upheavals). Taimur recalls a Sa'di tale his mother would tell him of a certain philosopher, Lukman, who is enslaved for a crime he did not commit. When the guilty party finally reveals himself many years later, the philosopher actually thanks his keeper, saying cryptically, "I have learned the only lesson worth learning about life, one that I would never have learned had you not imprisoned me" (383).

As his imaginative prowess evolves (much as Adie's crude Cavern simulations evolve, program by program, into the glorious superstructure of the Hagia Sophia), Taimur's constructions become more original, not merely restaged memories or borrowings from works he has read—they become the saving space of symbolic transaction.

Thus, Taimur evolves into an artist. One particularly affective reconstruction serves as important counterpoint to Adie's experiments within the Cavern. Even as Adie is mesmerized by the conjured Van Gogh painting in which she can "stand" at the half-opened window and "feel" the Provençal sun, Taimur reconstructs (again and again) a springtime stroll with Gwen through lakeside Chicago, a trip to the Art Institute where they had paused, mesmerized, before a similar Van Gogh painting, an actual experience recast as a verbal event and embellished (like all art) with symbolic layerings. With meticulous care, he reconstructs in language the perfect peace he felt at that moment, how the Provençal sunlight glowed on the canvas, how such sunshine "felt"—and the reader understands the power of the imagination, its ability to free the self from the press of the immediate and the ache of loneliness (Taimur, of course, is still chained to a radiator in Beirut). Importantly, the Van Gogh artifact, fashioned by a tormented and lonely hostage of a different sort more than a century earlier, had brought a moment's community to Gwen and Taimur: they had paused at the canvas and had set aside their usual bickering (he had earlier nearly hit her)—a respite that in turn extends now to Taimur and, of course, ultimately to the reader. After all, the artifact is still in the museum for anyone to share.

The imagination thus becomes an intricate strategy for connection; via the mesmerizing pull of Powers's prose, the reader "shares" the difficult isolation of the lonely Taimur. But, like all artists, Taimur (and Powers himself) conjures without an audience, save his own terrorized heart. Like all artists Taimur explores his soul, rekindles unsuspected internal energies, and draws strength from an imagination he had rarely engaged to make livable an oppressive immediate to which he knows he must return. Via the agency of language he unknowingly

PLOWING THE DARK

forges a community—in this case, with the reader. His captivity surely parallels the poignant interlude Adie spends with another artist-hostage, her ex-husband Ted Zimmerman, in the care facility in yet another Lebanon (in Ohio). There, similarly bound, strapped to his bed because his muscles lapse into uncontrollable spasms, and forced to endure the routine indignities of his deteriorating physical condition, Ted passes the time replaying memories and composing music at a specially designed computer keyboard, certain that such labor will not, indeed cannot, alter the difficult conditions of his reality but can make them endurable by shattering the difficult isolation he endures by projecting to an unnameable audience the rich melodies he hears in his head. Such is the very condition of the artist. Every poem, every novel, every painting, every melody is essentially done by the artist for the artist, a closed loop of conversation upon which fortunate others might eventually eavesdrop.

When the time comes at last for Taimur's negotiated release, the full dilemma of the aesthetic enterprise is made clear. For all the talk of the community with the audience, every artist is stubbornly unplaceable. At novel's end Taimur faces an uncertain reunion with Gwen, whom he learns has spearheaded the long struggle to secure his release. The reader surely wants a heartwarming Capraesque reunion as Taimur is shuttled out of Lebanon to (not coincidentally) Istanbul, there to meet not only Gwen but also a four-year-old daughter he has never met, who is that most difficult paradox, a loving stranger. Taimur struggles with the approaching moment, sensing how intrusive and uncertain love, even the tenderest and most sought after, can prove. For four years, he has bonded only with cockroaches and a scrawny mouse and briefly, by tapping on water pipes, with a fellow hostage. In the novel's last glimpse of Taimur, his daughter runs across the tarmac to meet him. She clutches a crayon drawing she has made for a father she has never seen, art offered one final time as a strategy for confluence among strangers. Will it work? If readers dare hope, they do so against the evidence. All the relationships in this novel detonate into disappointment. At one point, Adie follows the news story of Doris Singlegate, who agrees to live deprived of company in a chamber at the bottom of a mine shaft for two years. She fares well in isolation (she is championed in the media as the Mole-Woman). But she finds reentry difficult. Later it is revealed that she commits suicide.

Adie and Taimur then both close their narratives uneasily exposed, rudely deprived of the isolating environment in which so unexpectedly their aesthetic energies had been revived. Are they then the same sort of artist? What is the difference between the breathtaking spectacles within Adie's magic Cavern and Taimur's elaborate conjurings during his imprisonment? Consider first the environment from which they both retreat: the imperfect, often brutal real world. Consider Van Gogh's actual bedroom, to take one example Powers uses. Like all elements of the real world, that bedroom, located in an actual house in the south of France circa 1880, is subject to the intrusive agency of time. The Provençal sun that actually washed that tiny room passed with sobering quickness. The untidy arrangement of objects in that room, the accidental collision of shapes and colors, shifted daily. Thus, any reference to that room in France must be cased in the chilly past tense. And, like all the unspectacular objects—and persons—that animate the world, that room lacked meaning—save that it inexplicably sparked the restless, open eye of an isolate who retreated from the unmediated immediate long enough to record it using the relatively primitive medium of paint on stretched canvas.

PLOWING THE DARK

As an artifact, however, the bedroom significantly changes—the unremarkable suddenly becomes remarkable, the insignificant is suddenly freighted with unsuspected meaning, and the momentary becomes marvelously enduring. Suddenly the bedroom engages the eternal present tense. As an artifact, that room maintains its luster—creates an impact, becomes layered with argument, attains unexpected longevity—barring its deliberate destruction. And, most stunning, the lonely figure of Van Gogh working furiously with no expectation of audience manages to fashion a vast, indeed unlimited, community of other sensitive individuals who happen to come upon it, a confluence that has defied time and space. Those open to such an artifact are emotionally revived, the artifact able to provide the world what it so stubbornly lacks—depth. Such fortunate ones return from their encounter with this symbolic structure ready to engage the world more alert to themselves and their world and hence empowered despite the obvious: they are still subject to the bruising experiences that go along with the freewheeling ad-lib of living. What genuinely staggers Powers is the satisfying persistence of what is created, the effortless immortality available to such artifacts that, in turn, keep igniting the wholly accidental conspiracy of generations of responding "I's."

How much different, how much more disturbing, is the Cavern and, by extension, the stunning arrogance of virtual technology. One colleague rhapsodizes that cyberspace will be the new Stonehenge, a sublime place where twenty-first-century people can meet and feel part of something larger. But Powers resists such unexamined optimism. In the cool logic of withdrawal that defines the computer age, art is no longer an inviting, restorative place apart like Stonehenge. Such technology dismisses museums, libraries, theaters, concert halls as crudely literal; paper, canvas, even musical instruments can be dispensed with (a colleague plays on an invisible keyboard that sounds tones based on disturbances in the air). By insulating the individual within a simulated context that is as pliant as the original, cybergadgetry implicitly denies the negotiating at all with the imperfect immediate that has always been the ignition-site of art. Context is denied, text is everything. In the Cavern, *people* do not step into Van Gogh's bedroom—individuals do. In the long run, the engrossing spectacle effects concocted within such cool, engineered wombs merely create an appetite for deeper escapes, deeper diversions. No community is formed. Imagine a limitless private theme park, a sort of virtual Hobstown (Disney representatives are among those interested in investing in the Cavern). If traditional art generates a strategy in which the self is shared, cybertechnologies merely amplify the I.

Thus the privileged sanctuary of art becomes crudely literal. Pulled into such virtual environments, people too easily reject (like first-day theme park visitors) granting validity to the evident chaos of the real world. Powers cautions, however, that, as Adie notes when she opts to spend a day away from TeraSys and wanders about Seattle, "nothing beats sunlight" (161); recall when Adie assists Ted out into the sun porch of the care facility, his first venture outside in six months, and how compelling he finds the simple green of the trees. Within virtual realities, however, people can become accustomed to isolation, addicted to special effects. One TeraSys engineer, given entrance at age eleven to the comparatively crude escape of video games, passageways leading to passageways in an apparently unlimited adventure, some twenty years later, finds engaging the real world virtually impossible—he resigns his position at TeraSys after an Internet romance implodes when he actually meets the woman. Such is the future of the imagination. Powers suggests uneasily that virtual reality has only begun its impact—Adie foresees a time soon when virtual-reality environments will be enjoyed without the cumbersome goggles and clumsy wiring; rather, "billions of transistors" (267) would be surgically implanted in the brain, thus dispensing entirely with the need to engage the real world.

What is threatened, then, is the rich imaginative act itself, the space of symbolic transaction—the Van Gogh bedroom as reconjured by Taimur. It is, after all, strikingly different from the actual bedroom, the artifact in the museum, and Adie's three-dimensional simulation. Isolated, Taimur turns inward and there fashions a vision-narrative that exists, like all art, in the creative tension between autobiography and symbol, between memory and invention. Stunned by the artifact he finds entirely by accident in a museum, he now draws on that kinetic energy to console his brutalized self by fashioning on his own terms a wholly original take. It is the highest gesture of the imagination; it is the artist in each person, able to respond and to continue the aesthetic interplay by fashioning that response into a wholly private expression. Locked within the manifest untidiness of a brutal world, Taimur touches the consolation of the imagination. Never more alone, he is never more connected. He feels the swelling comfort of connection: to Gwen, to the artifact, to the long-dead troubled artist, to the legion others who have also felt the inexplicable response.

In the most luminous moment yet in Powers's fictions, he suggests the fabulous connection possible only within the aesthetic enterprise. He brings Adie and Taimur together. At the bleakest moment when Taimur assumes after three tedious years that his absurd captivity will never end, he feels momentarily tapped without any more stories to tell and pounds his forehead dully against the cell wall until it is bloody, closes his blindfolded eyes (doubling the darkness), and feels himself drop into an abyss. At that moment, he suddenly imagines a scene, which lasts no longer than a held breath, of a vast, richly detailed temple. Caught up in such an expanse, he walks about the interior, feels the generous bars of sunlight, and taps an unaccountable surge of hope. On impulse, he turns his eyes upward, and in the vast dome of the temple he spies a beautiful angel hanging for a moment before dropping down, not sweetly but in sheer terror over the precipitous drop. That inexplicable vision of the falling angel, so riveting and so mysterious, will sustain him for what will turn out to be another full year of confinement. When he is later pressed to explain how he survived so long, he cannot find words to articulate the consolation of the vision.

On the other side of the world, even as Taimur despairs, Adie is also undergoing the darkest moment in her soul. She has faced the difficult reality that military technology will co-opt the beauty of the Cavern. She has already destroyed much of the software she has helped build and is preparing to depart the project. But she dons the goggles for a last look about the Hagia Sophia, the masterwork of her time at TeraSys. Effortlessly, she steps into the vast sanctuary of the carefully detailed temple. She cues the wand and "soars" into the great dome. Suspended, she surveys the intricate interior she has fashioned—and spies in a terrifying moment a movement below, a shadow, a something there that she did not fashion. Startled, she clumsily shifts the wand and feels herself plummet earthward. Bewildered, haunted by the unprogrammed apparition, she will later tell her bemused colleagues that within their computer site is "something that wants out" (404). Feverish, she launches repeated efforts to "rescue" this shadow, but to no avail; her trips into that "private geometry" are as "tense and desperate as love" (405).

PLOWING THE DARK

What has transpired? Taimur and Adie, isolates, have met, defying the conventional logic of time and space. Powers audaciously approximates the sole reliable binding in a world where every transaction of the heart (back to *Three Farmers*) fails. It is the work of the imagination—not the heart—to provide the comfort of connection.[3] Adie and Taimur meet apart within the vast protective space of the imagination itself and each return, revived, to maintain their difficult positions within the aggressions, animosities, and ambivalences of the real world. Not that Powers endorses celibacy. Adie is consumed by the sheer pleasure of sensual exercise and Taimur longingly recalls intense sessions with Gwen. But such intensity inevitably ebbs. People need more. Sorrowful over the sorry decline of her once vibrant husband, Adie takes a cassette player into the woods outside Seattle and plays, as a sort of memorial service, a tape of her husband's favorite melody, the voluptuous seventeenth-century folk tune "Dives and Lazarus." Unexpectedly, from the depths of the woods, steps a stranger, a bearded lumberjack. The reader is immediately apprehensive over the encounter (Adie assumes she is trespassing). But the man merely pauses to relish the closing bars of the soulful tune and, before departing back into the darkness, thanks Adie. "I had forgotten that melody existed" (331). Two strangers, an artist and a lumberjack, unsponsored isolates from entirely different worlds, collide suddenly, inexplicably, wondrously within the fuselade world jury-rigged by a haunting melody more than three hundred years old. It is, paradoxically, a shared solitude, the elaborate trespass of the imagination, superior to any configuration the heart fashions and a binding simply not possible within the razzle-dazzle pleasure domes of virtual reality where fulfillment is designed only for one.

Powers, only in his mid-forties, is clearly at the top of his game, authoring in little more than fifteen years seven astonishing works that defiantly reject the massive cynicism, self-absorbed gamesmanship, and unearned despair that has defined so much contemporary serious fiction. With daring, Powers has reclaimed for the narrative art the ancient privilege of the imagination itself: to console, to exercise language (and Powers's prose is as compelling as the most luxuriant nineteenth-century reads) as a strategy to remind his reader that the difficult negotiations each person undergoes are still fit subject for recording. Trained to admire the elaborate lexical gamesplaying of postmodernism, Powers has nevertheless brought to the post-Pynchon era a humane vision largely because he understands that this is the work of literature: to enhance the experience by daring to affirm to readers whose lives may have been thinned by the corrosive effects of the twentieth century that, when they love passionately and clumsily, when they live inventing each moment from scratch, and when inevitably they concede to death, they participate in a millennia-old, species-wide drama, thus permitting them, if only for the moments they give over to reading, to escape the heavy burden of isolation that so defined existence in the uncertain close of the twentieth century. Escape and engagement finally are the same imperative. To borrow from Adie, the narratives people share break the terror of existence by depicting it.[4] Powers's novels cannot finally affirm meaning to life (that belongs to the lost conviction of religion) but they surely can fashion a community of both readers and characters who insist, against the evidence, that living—despite its evident imperfections—is capable of purpose, depth, expectation, and stunning shadow.

Like Emerson and Whitman more than a century ago, Powers understands that readers come to literature for affirmation. The earth,

PLOWING THE DARK

of course, can stun with its freewheeling wonder, but it cannot alleviate the darkling fears of mortality. The heart can fashion breathtaking connections, but it cannot promise that such bindings will not lapse into disappointment. It is finally the mysterious romance of art, the stirred imagination, that provides the sheltering interludes, the verbal/sonic/visual events that make possible the celebration of every moment, that remind the reader that the unexamined life is surely not worth the bother. He cannot bend to the hokey imperative of happy endings—he is too familiar with Emily Dickinson for that. He will not dispense sugar-pills for the anxious souls of the computer age. His characters can never quite shatter the hard carapace of the self. But neither must people relinquish delight. Rather within the aesthetic enterprise the reader comes to understand that every individual is part nevertheless of a vast, intricately patterned whole, each bit like the hard mineral grit that settles beautifully, accidentally, stunningly into quartz.

NOTES

Chapter One — Understanding Richard Powers

1. This is not to suggest that the novel of ideas is entirely extinct. Powers has repeatedly acknowledged his own admiration of two contemporary practitioners, Saul Bellow and Don DeLillo.

2. Directly quoted material in this chapter, unless otherwise noted, comes from a series of e-mail correspondences from Powers, dated 10 July, 14 July, and 23 Aug. 2000, and 8 Jan. 2001.

3. Powers has cited this respect in virtually every published interview, although he is careful to indicate that such professional admiration does not translate into direct influence. "This tag [of postmodernism] seems to be propagated by reviewers who read each other more than they read the novels in question. It's embarrassing and confusing. Five minutes with any page would show there's simply no comparison. Any reader who reads me in the hopes of finding that lineage is going to be deeply disappointed." Quoted in Neil Archer, "Mapping the Here and Now: An Interview with Richard Powers," *Tamaqua* 5, no. 2 (1995): 22.

4. Powers has never written in any genre save the novel. As he commented to me, "The short story lends itself . . . to an examination of life at eye level: how the world operates upon one or two or a small handful of sensibilities. The novel lends itself to the aerial view, a place for examining the ways that many intractable and irreducible sensibilities, thrown together, can operate on each other, and thereby build a world."

5. This lineage is striking if only because Powers so regularly alludes to both figures and yet the connection has never been explored. He told me, "I couldn't agree more with your desire to position me

along the axis you describe. You are onto something in my work that I've not seen elaborated or even hinted at elsewhere."

6. The change in course studies was a difficult one. Powers told me specifically the difficulty his father, Richard, had with the decision. His father valued literature, but not as a vocation. Powers still regrets that he was never able to "put a finished book in my father's hands"—Powers's father died from cancer just after Powers began graduate work. Of his mother, Donna, Powers recalls that she was a most adept housewife who had five children before she was 27. When the father's health failed, she kept the family together by "brushing up her high school secretarial skills and going into office work in her late thirties. I doubt that I would have even had the luxury of college had she not done so."

7. Quoted in Jeffrey Williams's on-line interview, "The Last Generalist: An Interview with Richard Powers," *Cultural Logic* 2, no. 2 (1999).

8. Quoted in Williams, "The Last Generalist."

9. Powers commented to me shortly after the publication of *Plowing the Dark,* "I see *Plowing the Dark* as a kind of end of the line for the kind of fiction I have been building up until now. What happens next will necessarily have to look quite a bit different."

10. When I asked about the interest in fairy tales, Powers responded, "Fairy tales play a recurrent, vital role in the shape and weight of my stories."

Chapter Two—*Three Farmers on Their Way to a Dance*

1. Richard Powers, *Three Farmers on Their Way to a Dance,* originally published 1985 (New York: Harper/Perennial, 1992), 16. All further references are noted parenthetically in the text.

2. Powers has frequently indicated that his empowering of the individual is framed by his own interest in chaos theory and particularly

NOTES TO PAGES 27–28

in the ramifications of the so-called Butterfly Effect, which posits the unsuspected impact that apparently random, minor events can have. See Janet Stites, "Bordercrossings: A Conversation in Cyberspace," *Omni* (Nov. 1993): 39–49.

3. Powers has indicated that this stereoscopic structure, which is helpfully explicated by James Hurt in "Narrative Powers: Richard Powers as Storyteller" (*Review of Contemporary Fiction* 18, no. 3 [1998]), is indebted to Joyce and *Ulysses:* "He told this absolutely dense realistic story.... But parallel to that was a frame completely contiguous to the first, and yet a kind of intellectual commentary on it. . . . This notion that you can produce three dimensions out of two complementary planes was the one I subsequently picked up on and tried to work with in *Three Farmers*." Quoted in Sven Birkerts, "An Interview with Richard Powers," *Bomb* (summer 1998): 60.

4. Preston Sturges directed a series of stunningly popular screwball comedies in the 1940s in which improbable events, propelled by coincidence and luck, move two central characters toward the realization of true love and thus toward a happy ending. Given Powers's interest in classic films, the possibility of his deliberately tapping into that formula is quite real. Hurt argues that this plotline is reminiscent of 1930s comedies ("Narrative Powers," 26).

5. Powers has frequently cited the impact of aesthetic theoretician Walter Benjamin and specifically his groundbreaking essay, "The Work of Art in the Age of Mechanical Reproduction." Chapter 19, "The Cheap and Accessible Print," is the narrator's extended commentary on the implications of Benjamin's thesis on the "strange persuasion of photography" and the aesthetic implications of the ability to reproduce "limitless, virtually identical images" (253). For extended analysis of Benjamin and the argument of Powers's first novel, see Greg Dawes, "The Storm of Progress: *Three Farmers on Their Way to a Dance*," *Review of Contemporary Fiction* 18, no. 3 (1998): 42–50.

6. Powers has termed it "youthful exuberance" (see Birkerts, "An Interview with Richard Powers," 61) and admits that "something

about the optimism and naked assertion of [that novel] still makes me wince a little" (quoted in Jim Neilson, "An Interview with Richard Powers," *Review of Contemporary Fiction* 18, no. 3 [1998]: 14).

Chapter Three—*Prisoner's Dilemma*

1. Richard Powers, *Prisoner's Dilemma* (New York: Beech Tree/Morrow, 1988), 19. Further references to this book are noted parenthetically in the text.

2. In his seminal review of *Prisoner's Dilemma* Tom LeClair focuses on the novel's use of chaos theory as a structuring device, as a way for Powers—and other novelists including Gaddis, DeLillo, Barth, and Pynchon—to reveal "richly specified little people whose lives trickle into the large motions of history" ("The Systems Novel," *The New Republic*, 25 Apr. 1988, 41).

3. The term "pleasure prison" is a particularly apt phrase deployed by LeClair in his review of the novel.

4. Interestingly, Powers published Eddie's chapter separately as "The Best Place for It" (*New Yorker*, 1 Feb. 1988, 28–35). The title, from Robert Frost's "Birches," suggests Eddie's ability to affirm the unsuspected grace of the imperfect world.

5. Despite the critical interest in Powers as an obsessive analyst of laboratory science and a technowonk, he indicated to me that "the force that drives the fuse" in his books is "definitely green" (e-mail correspondence, 14 July 2000).

6. For a different take see Arthur Saltzman's reading of the novel's close. Saltzman accepts the dead father's return as a triumph of art over the real world. Powers could not restore his own father; thus he brings back his character as a gesture of reprieve. "The Poetics of Elsewhere: *Prisoner's Dilemma* and *The MacGuffin*," in *The Novel in the Balance* (Columbia: University of South Carolina Press, 1993), 109.

NOTES TO PAGES 50–56

Chapter Four—*The Gold Bug Variations*

1. Hyperbole dominated the critical response. In addition to *Time*'s recognition of the book as its novel of the year, Louis Jones in *The New York Times Book Review* (25 Aug. 1991, 9–10) hailed its "stunning virtuosity." Curt Suplee in *The Washington Post* (25 Aug. 1991, 5) compared it to nothing less than *Moby-Dick; Publishers Weekly* doubted that the decade, only a year old, would "bring another novel half as challenging and original" (14 June 1991, 44). *Kirkus Reviews* (1 June 1991, 689) dubbed it a "formidable masterpiece," and Paula LaRocque of the *Dallas Morning News* (20 Oct. 1991, J6+) predicted the book would take its place "among the classics of American literature." Carlin Romano (*Philadelphia Inquirer*, 8 Sept. 1991, D11+) hailed it as "the most important and intellectually challenging American novel of the year." Powers himself has cited the book as his most satisfying endeavor (quoted in Birkerts interview, 61). In "The Prodigious Fiction of Richard Powers, William Vollman, and David Foster Wallace," *Critique* 38, no. 1 (fall 1996): 12–37, Tom LeClair used *Gold Bug* as occasion to declare Powers a massively gifted prodigy.

2. Richard Powers, *The Gold Bug Variations* (New York: Morrow, 1991), 324. Further references to this novel are noted parenthetically in the text.

3. See Scott Hermanson, "Chaos and Complexity in Richard Powers's *The Gold Bug Variations*," *Critique* 38, no. 1 (1996): 38–52, which elegantly applies chaos theory to the novel as a narrative structure and concludes that the novel offers a fractal design in which reiterated events create a stunning design.

4. Labinger (85–90) does a most sensitive job of reviewing how intricately the novel follows the plan of Bach's keyboard exercise (see Jay Labinger, "Encoding an Infinite Message: Richard Powers's *The Gold Bug Variations*," *Configurations* 3, no. 1 [1995]). Hurt ("Narrative Powers," 34–37) reviews the novel's polyphonic organization as well.

5. I have argued elsewhere ("'Hooking the Nose of the Leviathan': Information, Knowledge, and the Mystery of Bonding in *The Gold Bug Variations*," *Review of Contemporary Fiction* 18, no. 3 [1998], 59–61) that the tension in the novel between engaging life and retreating from its bruising experience is related metaphorically to Ressler's notion that to crack protein sequencing scientists would need to simulate the molecular activity in vitro, that no understanding would be possible in vivo. Powers suggests understanding life is far easier removed from the ongoing, unfolding process itself. The tension between heart and head is explicit in the novel's pun that splices Bach's formidable aesthetic achievement with Poe's celebration of the rational faculty, a mystery story passed among the members of the university research project.

Chapter Five—*Operation Wandering Soul*

1. Richard Powers, *Operation Wandering Soul* (New York: Morrow, 1993), 17. Further references to this novel are noted parenthetically in the text.

2. Cancer forms something of a compelling motif in Powers's fictions; he has often indicated that a number of close friends—and his father—have died from the disease. Its unstoppable intrusion is used in each of his novels to suggest the urgent energy of the natural world and our vulnerabilities within it. In his latest novel, *Plowing the Dark,* Powers uses multiple sclerosis to suggest this idea.

3. In an Internet dialogue with novelist Bradford Morrow, Powers recalls the moment the organizing frame of the novel struck him. Touring Germany on a rail pass, Powers stopped in Hamelin and happened upon a wall plaque that commemorated the street down which the children had disappeared in 1284. "That instantly triggered the memory of my brother's account of serving as surgical resident in a large Los Angeles hospital ER on the afternoon when a killer opened

fire in a nearby grade school playground." See "A Dialogue: Richard Powers and Bradford Morrow," *Conjunctions* 34: *American Fiction: States of the Art* (spring 2000).

4. Initial critical response largely accepted Kraft as Powers's voice and, not surprisingly, found the book forbiddingly apocalyptic and excessively bleak. See John Skow, "Children's Ward," *Time,* 19 July 1993, 64–66, and Cleo Kearns, "The Harrowing Grace of Truthful Fiction," *Theology Today,* Jan. 1995, 588–93. Meg Wolitzer (*New York Times Book Review,* 18 July 1993, 19) indicts the novel for its excessive prose but never considers the possibility Powers is creating a manic voice. That "Kraft" translates loosely from the German "power" may be less suggestive of parallels to the author and more suggestive of the character's helplessness and his agonizing need to assert some measure of control amid what he sees as unstoppable forces.

5. Powers describes the style as "completely over the top, a verbal mania that is supposed to reflect Richard Kraft's increasingly apocalyptic read on inner-city Los Angeles" (quoted by Neilson in "An Interview with Richard Powers," 20).

6. See Hurt's insightful analysis of this narrative technique in "Narrative Powers," 38–40.

7. The angel charm she wears might suggest a further intriguing tie with Kraft. His father, during the American helicopter raids over Laos, helped toss such charms down onto the villages. Joy tells Kraft that her charm fell out of the sky.

8. Lindner ("Narrative as Necessary Evil in Richard Powers's *Operation Wandering Soul*," *Critique* 38, no. 1 [1996]: 68–80) makes the opposite point—that here Powers affirms the narrative as a way of ordering the chaos of the world, a necessary anesthetic against harsh reality. This again accepts Kraft as Powers's mouthpiece, an assumption called into question by the text, by Powers himself, and by all Powers's other works that resist just such pessimism.

NOTES TO PAGES 91–100

Chapter Six—*Galatea 2.2*

1. In an interview that coincided with the novel's publication Powers spoke to this interaction as the central dynamic of the book: "In trying to narrate the shape of the betraying world to a disembodied piece of machinery, [Richard Powers] recovers, again, the inexplicable density of assumptions about the outside world that the mind must repeatedly make and unmake. . . . The easiest, most assimilated facts of our existence would blow us away with their complexity if we stopped for a moment to consider them." Quoted by Neil Archer in "Mapping the Here and Now," 13, 15.

2. Richard Powers, *Galatea 2.2* (New York: Farrar, Straus and Giroux, 1995), 202. Further references to this book are noted parenthetically in the text.

3. The character is given to similar extravagant emotional responses that are both melodramatic and overwrought. When colleagues play a rather minor practical joke on him, he determines that he will never again trust anybody. He obsesses over the beautiful graduate student, including accessing her university records and shadowing her as she goes to class. His determination to abandon writing is surely a most grand gesture. Such extravagant gestures indicate a character radically uncomfortable with normative human interaction and simple emotional expression. N. Katherine Hayles in her brief discussion of the novel (*How We Became Posthuman: Virtual Bodies in Cybernetics, Literature, and Informatics* [Berkeley: University of California Press, 1999]) works out ways in which the novel uses doubling, characters reflecting one another, and makes the point that the character Richard Powers is clearly not its author and that we are asked to scrutinize his behavior and his tendency to melodrama.

4. See Arthur Saltzman's insightful treatment of the novel for a careful delineation of the metaphoric and thematic implication of each successive implementation leading up to Helen. "The Trope in the Machine" in *This Mad "Instead": Governing Metaphors in Contemporary*

NOTES TO PAGES 101-120

American Fiction (Columbia: University of South Carolina Press, 2000), 94–109.

5. In the Berube interview Powers speaks of the novel as an "interrogation of parenthood" (Michael Berube, "Urbana Renewal: A Conversation with the Powers That Be," *Voice Literary Supplement,* 6 June 1995, 8).

Chapter Seven—*Gain*

1. Reviews cited Laura as ordinary and her storyline as strikingly pedestrian. John Updike ("Soap and Death in America," *New Yorker,* 27 July 1998) called the storyline "sitcomish" and a "medical weepie" (77). Tom LeClair ("Powers of Invention," *The Nation,* 27 July/3 Aug. 1998) termed the storyline as "soap opera" (34). Michiko Kakutani (*New York Times,* 11 Aug. 1998, E6) cited the Clare narrative as the novel's achievement, interrupted by Laura's "dreary history." Even A. O. Scott, in an extensive *New York Review of Books* piece, acknowledged that the novel moved back and forth from a "made-for-TV movie" to an episode of *Nova* ("A Matter of Life and Death," 17 Dec. 1998, 40).

2. Initial reviews did not find such affirmation. Updike found the book "cold," the prose not so much written as "administered" ("Soap and Death," 77). Kakutani dismissed Laura's narrative as dreary and the Clare chronicle as predictable in its depiction of greed. Scott sensed the hopefulness in the narrative but never dealt explicitly with the Whitman tie. Rather he found Powers "oddly hopeful and humane" ("A Matter of Life and Death," 42).

3. Richard Powers, *Gain* (New York: Farrar, Straus and Giroux, 1998), 87. Further references to this novel are noted parenthetically in the text.

4. Updike and Kakutani both found the novel too lesson-driven and found Powers, for all his intelligence, offering a thin theme: greed

is bad. But Powers himself has often made the point that *Gain,* if it is to succeed as art rather than as polemic, had to balance its approach to corporate responsibility. See particularly his on-line interview with Jeffrey Williams ("The Last Generalist") and his *Bomb* interview with Birkerts ("An Interview with Richard Powers").

5. Charles B. Harris ("'The Stereo View': Politics and the Role of the Reader in *Gain,*" *Review of Contemporary Fiction* 18, no. 3 [1998]: 97–108) has a considerably different take on this closing section. He suggests that the novel's larger pessimism is underscored by this section, in which Laura herself is commodified and becomes another processed thing. It is a difficult reading to accept given the stirring closing days of Laura's life and given the sweep of Powers's fiction, which finds technology/science and its creator-species more cooperative than combative.

Chapter Eight—*Plowing the Dark*

1. See Powers's on-line interview, given in connection with the release of *Plowing the Dark,* with *Esquire* literary critic Sven Birkerts: "My apology for fiction has always taken the form of saying: When we live in real time, under the onslaught of the challenges of unmediated existence, we cannot solve all the problems that are thrown at us. . . . Therefore we remove ourselves into the space of symbolic transaction. . . . And then we reenter, more equipped, the world of reality" ("The *Esquire* Conversation with Richard Powers," *Esquire,* July 2000, 46, 49; Internet posting at http://www.esquire.com/needto-know/books/ooo701–mfe-powers03.html, accessed August 2000).

2. Richard Powers, *Plowing the Dark* (New York: Farrar, Straus and Giroux, 2000), 265. Further references to this novel are noted parenthetically in the text.

3. Critical response was divided on how to take this gesture. The division of course reflects Powers's Dickinsonesque take on the imagination

NOTES TO PAGE 148

as cool consolation. Daniel Zalewski, for example, cites such consolation as chilling, "an empty sort of razzle-dazzle" ("Actual Reality," *New York Times Book Review,* 18 June 2000, 12). Although he finds the collision of Adie and Taimur within the invention of the Hagia Sophia "riveting," he finds the offer of the imagination to be too "sentimental." Steven Moore, however, finds it "emotionally powerful" ("Virtual Artistry," *Washington Post Book World,* 4 June 2000, 6).

4. Interestingly, in *Plowing the Dark,* the dying composer, Ted Zimmerman, had suffered at the hands of elitist New York music critics when he dared to compose on commission a musical piece that recalled traditional tonality and harmonics, a composition that defied conventional postmodern dicta of experimental (and largely unlistenable) music, a composition that was shockingly unshocking. There is indeed in Powers's fiction a similar return to the traditional dictums of realistic novels and a tempering of the shock tactics and the experimental imperatives of postmodern writing.

BIBLIOGRAPHY

Works by Richard Powers

Books

Three Farmers on Their Way to a Dance. New York: Beech Tree/Morrow, 1985. London: Weidenfeld and Nicolson, 1988.

Prisoner's Dilemma. New York: Beech Tree/Morrow, 1988. London: Weidenfeld and Nicolson, 1989.

The Gold Bug Variations. New York: Morrow, 1991. London: Abacus, 1993.

Operation Wandering Soul. New York: Morrow, 1993. London: Abacus, 1994.

Galatea 2.2: A Novel. New York: Farrar, Straus and Giroux, 1995. London: Abacus, 1996.

Gain. New York: Farrar, Straus and Giroux, 1998. London: Heinemann, 2000.

Plowing the Dark. New York: Farrar, Straus and Giroux, 2000. London: Heinemann, 2001.

Articles

"State and Vine." *Yale Review* 79, no. 2 (1990): 690–98. Essay-review of Thomas Pynchon's *Vineland*.

"A Game We Couldn't Lose." *New York Times,* 18 Feb. 1996, IV 13. Op-ed piece that examines both the humanist and the technologist arguments on the ballyhooed showdown between chessmaster Gary Kasparov and IBM's Deep Blue computer.

"Losing Our Souls, Bit by Bit." *New York Times,* 15 July 1998, A19. Editorial about diminishing privacy in the information age.

"Life by Design: Too Many Breakthroughs." *New York Times,* 19 Nov. 1998, A32. A cautionary op-ed piece on the potential problems from the careless and speedy application of the theories of biotechnology.

"Eyes Wide Open." *New York Times Magazine,* 18 Apr. 1999, 80–83. Cites as the most important idea of the closing millennium the largely unknown work of a tenth-century Iraqi theoretician, Ibn al-Haytham, who in an effort to explain the mystery of vision first championed the value of scientific investigation and controlled experimentation.

"American Dreaming: The Limitless Absurdity of Our Belief in an Infinitely Transformable Future." *New York Times Magazine,* 7 May 2000, 67. A conservative, eloquent caution to a survey in which contemporary American culture, lured by the promise of technology and the great strides of the last century, stakes considerable faith in the idea that virtually any future is available.

Selected Works about Richard Powers

Web Sites

Dodd, David. "Richard Powers: A Bibliography." Available from http://arts.ucsc.edu/GDead/AGDL/powers.html. A reliable, thorough, and regularly updated listing of reviews and publications on Powers.

Interviews

Archer, Neil. "Mapping the Here and Now: An Interview with Richard Powers." *Tamaqua* 5, no. 2 (1995): 10–23.

BIBLIOGRAPHY

Berube, Michael. "Urbana Renewal: A Conversation with the Powers That Be." *Voice Literary Supplement,* 6 June 1995, 8–10. An intriguing experiment in metainterviewing conducted between Richard Powers, the writer of *Galatea 2.2,* and Richard Powers, the character in *Galatea 2.2.*

Birkerts, Sven. "An Interview with Richard Powers." *Bomb* (summer 1998): 59–63. Intelligent, absorbing interview that reviews biographical background on Powers, his structural use of music, his concept of using a novel to investigate questions raised by the previous work, and his ideas about narrative as a response to crisis in the technological age.

———. "The *Esquire* Conversation with Richard Powers." *Esquire,* July 2000, 46, 49. Available from http://www.esquire.com/needtoknow/books/ooo701–mfe-powers03.html. Accessed August 2000.

"A Dialogue: Richard Powers and Bradford Morrow." *Conjunctions* 34: *American Fiction: States of the Art* (spring 2000). Available from http://www.conjunctions.com/archives/c34–rp.htm. An e-mail dialogue between two novelists (and friends) of the post-Pynchon era. Fascinating and informative insights on the process of writing, the importance of narrative in an age of easy cynicism, and the impact of being an novelist on the role of reader.

Neilson, Jim. "An Interview with Richard Powers." *Review of Contemporary Fiction* 18, no. 3 (1998): 13–23.

Stites, Janet. "Bordercrossings: A Conversation in Cyberspace." *Omni* (Nov. 1993): 39–49. An important dialogue executed via e-mail among Powers, University of California at Los Angeles literary critic N. Katherine Hayles, and California Institute of Technology chemistry professor Jay Labinger. Intriguing and often dense theorizing on the softening boundaries between science and literature, specifically the influence of chaos theory on contemporary fiction.

Williams, Jeffrey. "The Last Generalist: An Interview with Richard Powers." *Cultural Logic* 2, no. 2 (1999). Available from

BIBLIOGRAPHY

http://www.eserver.org/clogic/2-2. An especially strong interview that, although focused on *Gain,* reviews Powers's ideas about the function of the novel, the role of literary criticism, and the participatory aspect of the reading experience. Includes helpful biographical information.

Selected Critical Analyses

Birkerts, Sven. "Mapping the New Reality: American Fictions." *Wilson Quarterly* 16, no. 2 (1992): 102–10. Argues that contemporary realism has largely failed to grapple with the implications of the cyber-age with the exception of the paranoids (conspiracy theorists and system novelists such as DeLillo and Mailer) and the intellectuals (such as Powers), who seek not to depict the era but to understand the concept-driven world engendered by the sciences.

Dawes, Greg. "The Storm of Progress: *Three Farmers on Their Way to a Dance.*" *Review of Contemporary Fiction* 18, no. 3 (1998): 42–50. Extended analysis of Walter Benjamin's theories as they relate to *Three Farmers on Their Way to a Dance.*

Dewey, Joseph. "Dwelling in Possibility: The Fiction of Richard Powers." *The Hollins Critic* 33, no. 2 (1996): 2–16. The first assessment of Powers's fiction as a thematic whole (through *Galatea 2.2*). Develops a rubric of the head, the heart, and the imagination as strategies for engaging a brutal twentieth-century world. Uses Powers's interest in Emily Dickinson as thematic guide.

———. "'Hooking the Nose of the Leviathan': Information, Knowledge, and the Mystery of Bonding in *The Gold Bug Variations.*" *Review of Contemporary Fiction* 18, no. 3 (1998): 51–66.

———. "Humming the (In)Sufficient Heart Out: Richard Powers' *The Gold Bug Variations.*" In *Novels from Reagan's America: A New Realism,* 223–50. Gainesville: University Press of Florida, 1999.

BIBLIOGRAPHY

Uses *The Gold Bug Variations* as capstone text in a cultural investigation into a revolutionary redefinition of the agenda and vision of American literary realism during the Reagan era.

Hermanson, Scott. "Chaos and Complexity in Richard Powers's *The Gold Bug Variations*." *Critique* 38, no. 1 (1996): 38–52. Explores how Powers uses the implications of chaos theory to create a love story patterned on nonlinear dynamics (specifically the structural use of chance and recursive iterations and the themes of the unsuspected importance of the individual and the necessary mystery of nature).

Hurt, James. "Narrative Powers: Richard Powers as Storyteller." *Review of Contemporary Fiction* 18, no. 3 (1998): 24–41. A solid introduction to Powers's first four novels with particular attention to their interlocking narrative structuring. Argues that Powers's gift as storyteller revives the "much-maligned" art of ordering a chaotic world through the therapy of plot.

Labinger, Jay. "Encoding an Infinite Message: Richard Powers's *The Gold Bug Variations*." *Configurations* 3, no. 1 (1995): 79–93. A fascinating structuralist reading that documents the tight unity of Powers's novel by deploying different uses of coding—computer codes, genetic codes, the generating code of Bach's keyboard works, and even language itself. Includes a valuable working out (with schematics) of the contrapuntal narrative lines. Indispensable.

LeClair, Tom. "The Prodigious Fiction of Richard Powers, William Vollman, and David Foster Wallace." *Critique* 38, no. 1 (fall 1996): 12–37. An important reading of *The Gold Bug Variations* by an early and eloquent proponent of Powers. Places Powers within the post-postmodern tradition of young brainy authors— fascinated by information, by computers, and by science—who, in turn, produce massive texts that seek nothing less than the description of the mysterious extravagance of life itself.

BIBLIOGRAPHY

———. "The Systems Novel." *New Republic* (25 Apr. 1988): 40–42. Focuses on chaos theory as a structuring device in *Prisoner's Dilemma* and in works by other novelists.

Lindner, April. "Narrative as Necessary Evil in Richard Powers's *Operation Wandering Soul*." *Critique* 38, no. 1 (1996): 68–80. Examines the novel as metafiction, specifically an absorbing realistic narrative that undermines itself. Like a fairy tale, such a gripping narrative provides the reader/child with placating structures of order and thus maintains contentment (and preserves the status quo) in a chaotic "world that calls for outrage and action."

Marsh, Kelly A. "The Neo-Sensation Novel: A Contemporary Genre in the Victorian Tradition." *Philological Quarterly* 74, no. 1 (1995): 99–123. A not entirely convincing reading of *The Gold Bug Variations* as one example of contemporary novels that rework the Victorian romance/gothic genre of novels about secrets: plot-heavy novels designed to intrigue readers by the unfolding process of discovery. Uses *Bleak House* as comparison.

Saltzman, Arthur M. "The Poetics of Elsewhere: *Prisoner's Dilemma* and *The MacGuffin*." In *The Novel in the Balance*, 103–12. Columbia: University of South Carolina Press, 1993. A lucid, close reading of Powers's second novel as a postmodern construct that explores the balance between escape/flight and engagement/accommodation and the consequent struggle to live within the brutal twentieth century without seductive imaginative refuges.

———. "The Trope in the Machine." In *This Mad "Instead": Governing Metaphors in Contemporary American Fiction*, 94–109. Columbia: University of South Carolina Press, 2000. An insightful discussion of metaphors in *Galatea 2.2*.

Scott, A. O. "A Matter of Life and Death." Review of *Gain*. *New York Review of Books*, 17 Dec. 1998, 38, 40–42. A compelling response to *Gain* as an example of American novels about business. Finds

BIBLIOGRAPHY

that, although Powers has the "disturbing braininess" and "taste for narrative experimenting" that defines Thomas Pynchon, he is, at heart, a realist who is "disarmingly emotional" and not afraid of "moral passion."

Snyder, Sharon. "The Gender of Genius: Scientific Experts and Literary Amateurs in the Fiction of Richard Powers." *Review of Contemporary Fiction* 18, no. 3 (1998): 84–96. Argues that in *The Gold Bug Variations* Powers defies conventional fiction by using a female character as scientist/researcher figure and as model for the scientific virtues of amateur investigation, inspiration, and collaboration.

Updike, John. "Novel Thoughts." Review of *Galatea 2.2. New Yorker*, 21/28 Aug. 1995, 105–14. Oft-cited appreciation of Powers's fifth novel, lauding its ability to return fiction to its highest philosophical imperative: to make readers ponder age-old metaphysical questions even as they are emotionally involved with the unfolding narrative.

INDEX

Alice in Wonderland (Carroll), 79, 81

Barth, John, 3, 154
Benjamin, Walter, 153
Berkeley, Busby, 37
Bernard of Clairvaux, 101
Bellow, Saul, 151
Brueghel, Peter, 63

Cervantes, Miguel de, 100
chaos theory, 35, 133, 152, 155
Cheever, John, 3
A Christmas Carol (Dickens), 37, 41

Dalhart, Vernon, 41
Darwin, Charles, 7, 48
Decameron (Boccaccio), 32, 36
DeLillo, Don, 151, 154
Dickinson, Emily, 5, 6, 9, 12, 28, 34–35, 50, 57, 59, 61, 67, 78, 99, 131, 148–49, 160
Dickens, Charles, 133, 138. *See also A Christmas Carol*
Disney, Walt, 9, 31–32, 33–37, 42, 44, 48–49, 79, 82–83, 88–89, 113, 124, 144
"Dives and Lazarus" (folk song), 147

Ellison, Ralph, 103
Emerson, Ralph Waldo, 5, 6, 9, 12, 16, 22, 24, 26–28, 35, 41–45, 47, 50, 52, 65, 70, 74, 83, 106, 120, 148

Fantasia (Disney film), 31, 37, 44
Frank, Anne, 82, 85

INDEX

Frankenstein (Shelley), 99, 102, 103
Frost, Robert, 138, 154

Gaddis, William, 3, 154
Gass, William, 3
The Goldberg Variations (Bach) 51, 54, 55–56, 60, 61, 64, 66, 67, 113, 155–56, 173
Gone with the Wind (Mitchell), 37
Gould, Glenn, 54, 60

Hardy, Thomas, 7
Hobstown, 72, 73, 82, 88, 94, 97, 105, 113, 123, 127. *See also Prisoner's Dilemma*
Homer, 95–6

The Iliad (Homer), 7, 151
It's a Wonderful Life (Capra film) 31, 37, 41, 44, 48, 124, 141

Jack and the Beanstalk, 13, 20, 22, 25, 27, 53, 75–76
Joyce, James, 7, 95, 153

Kipling, Rudyard, 48

Mahler, Gustav, 60
Mann, Thomas, 7
Moby-Dick (Melville), 5, 35, 155

Newton, Isaac, 38

The Odyssey (Homer), 7
O'Hara, John, 3
Orchestra Wives (film), 37

INDEX

Peter Pan, 7, 71, 75, 81, 84
Pied Piper, 13, 71, 72, 82, 156–57
Pinocchio, 98, 102–3
Poe, Edgar Allan, 58, 156
postmodernism, 3, 4, 33–34, 80, 96, 148, 151, 161
Powers, Richard, biography of, 6–10; computer sciences in works of, 5, 8, 50, 58–59, 65, 90, 92, 99–106, 127, 131–32, 134–35, 143–45, 147; definition of imagination in works of, 2–3, 10, 11–14, 15–17, 22–29, 32, 34–35, 41, 45–52, 67–75, 79–88; history as theme in works of, 12, 23, 42, 30, 32, 33, 35–36, 73, 79; the individual in the works of, 13, 25, 41, 68–69, 128–29; knowledge as theme in works of, 1,2, 22–24, 38–39, 57–58, 61, 84, 99, 101; loneliness in works of, 1, 5, 11–14, 15–16, 22–28, 41–42, 52–53, 61–62, 74, 78, 85, 89, 92–96, 101, 131–32, 140, 148; love as theme in works of, 1,2, 19, 22, 24, 39, 43–44, 53–59, 60–64, 67–69, 77–78, 84–89, 96, 141–42, 147, 149; nature as theme in works of, 44–45, 52, 58, 60–61, 69, 83, 85, 112, 114–21, 125, 128–29, 148–49; optimism as theme in works of, 3–14, 68–70, 74–76, 83–87, 108–9, 114, 124–29, 133, 145–46, 148–49, 153–54, 159; polyphonic narratives structures in fiction of, 11–12, 15–16, 21–22, 26–28, 29–30, 33, 37–38, 53–55, 62–63, 67–68, 81–82, 86–87, 90, 95, 110–12, 132–34, 136; science in works of, 7–13, 44–45, 52–59, 61, 73–76, 112–19, 120–27; use of children's stories in works of, 13, 24, 72, 81, 82, 85, 88, 99–100, 152

Novels

Gain, 4, 9, 12, 110–29, 130, 134, 159–60; and death, 112–15, 116–19, 123–29; and the problem with disengagement, 112–13, 123–24; and science and technology, 118–19, 122–23, 125, 127; as education narrative, 118–20, 126–29; as realistic narrative, 110–12; nature in, 112–16, 121, 122–28; optimism in, 128–29

Galatea 2.2, 9, 12, 89–109, 123, 159–60; and the failure of love, 92–97,100–104; and the limits of language, 97–99, 100–101,

105–6; as autobiographical work, 94–95, 158; as defense of the imagination, 90–91, 95–100, 102–3; as fairy tale, 99–100; definition of writer in, 107–8; engagement as solution in, 104–8

The Gold Bug Variations, 4, 9, 12, 50–70, 71, 73, 74, 78, 113, 122, 155–56; and genetics, 52–58, 63–68; and language, 64, 67–68; as polyphonic narrative, 53–56, 67–68; connection as theme in, 62–69; desire as theme in, 56–61, 67

Operation Wandering Soul, 4, 9, 12, 70–88, 89–90,156–57; and children's stories, 71–77; 83–86; and denial of spiritual, 72, 76–78; and pessimism, 73–79, 82, 86; and theme of acceptance, 83–85, 87, 88; as told-narrative, 74–76, 81–82, 86–88; excessive style in, 74–76, 157; retreat as strategy in, 79–81, 86–87

Plowing the Dark, 9, 12, 130–49, 152, 160–61; and theme of art, 130–36, 140–42, 143; definition of the imagination in, 131–37, 140–46; relationship of art to the real world as theme in, 142, 144–45, 143; theme of connection in, 145–47, 148–45

Prisoner's Dilemma, 4, 9, 12, 29–49, 51, 69, 73, 82, 112, 154; and nature, 44–45; and strategy of withdrawal, 129, 135–41; and theme of engagement, 46–49; as Emersonian argument 41–45; as response to nuclear war, 36–37; narrative design in, 33–38, 45–47. *See also* Hobstown

Three Farmers on Their Way to a Dance, 4, 8, 12, 15–28, 29, 32, 33, 34, 37, 46, 47, 49, 50, 69, 88, 89, 117, 147, 152–54; as Emersonian argument, 26–28; as reclamation narrative, 22–24; definition of the individual in, 24–25; narrative structure in, 21–22, 26–27; open ending of, 26–28; role of the reader in, 27; use of the imagination in, 26–28

The Time of Our Singing, 10

Major Characters

(discussions of the character other than in the relevant chapter)
Laura Bodey (*Gain*), 130, 159–60

INDEX

Eddie Hobson (*Prisoner's Dilemma*), 51, 52, 61, 68, 70, 73, 74, 79, 86, 89, 90, 91, 98, 103, 105, 106, 110, 114, 117, 124
Eddie Hobson Jr. (*Prisoner's Dilemma*), 51, 53, 57–8, 65, 76, 83, 84, 85, 100, 105
Richard Kraft (*Operation Wandering Soul*), 89, 90, 91, 98, 103, 106, 108, 157
Nameless narrator (*Three Farmers on Their Way to a Dance*), 32, 35, 43, 52, 107, 110, 130
Jan O'Deigh (*The Gold Bug Variations*), 89, 100
Richard Powers (*Galatea 2.2*), 110, 113, 129, 158
Stuart Ressler (*The Gold Bug Variations*), 74, 76, 78, 81, 83, 84, 85, 89, 90, 98, 103, 105, 106, 110, 114, 117, 121, 127
Joy Stepaneevong (*Operation Wandering Soul*), 110, 114, 117

"The Prisoner's Song," 41
Proust, Marcel, 7
Pygmalion, 9, 90, 100, 101, 102–3
Pynchon, Thomas, 3, 10, 95, 148, 151, 154

realism, 3, 4, 7, 13, 33, 110–11, 148, 161
Rousseau, Henri, 134, 136

Sa'di, 133, 139
Sander, August, 8, 16, 17, 18, 19, 25, 26, 28, 97
Sargent, John Singer, 137
The Scarlet Letter (Hawthorne), 5, 22, 27
Schneider, Robert, 7
Schoenberg, Arthur, 133
Snow White, 13, 34, 35, 39, 41, 53, 75, 76
Sturges, Preston, 27, 153
Styron, William, 3

The Tempest (Shakespeare), 102, 106

INDEX

Thomas, Dylan, 113
Twain, Mark, 103

Updike, John, 3,5, 159

Van Gogh, Vincent, 133–34, 140–45

Where the Wild Things Are (Sendak), 13, 107–8
Whitman, Walt, 12, 42, 52, 70, 83, 114–19, 126, 128–29, 159
The Wizard of Oz (film and Baum book), 37, 48, 79, 81
Wolff, Harold, 48
Wright, Richard, 103

Yeats, William Butler, 102, 134, 135, 139

www.ingramcontent.com/pod-product-compliance
Lightning Source LLC
Chambersburg PA
CBHW020232170426
43201CB00007B/405